The Tender Trap

THE MAN WITH THE GOLDEN ARM

Pal Joey

COME BLOW YOUR HORN

M-G-M's "TILL THE CLOUDS ROLL BY"

THE JOKER IS WILD"

"The Kissing Bandit"

In HiGH Society

THE DETECTIVE

Take Me Out to the Ball Game

THE MANCHURIAN CANDIDATE

"DOUBLE DYNAMITE"

TONY ROME

Von Ryan's

THE CINEMATIC LEGACY OF
FRANK SINATRA

DAVID WILLS

Contributing Essays by

NANCY SINATRA, TINA SINATRA, and FRANK SINATRA, JR.

Contributing Photo Editor

AMANDA ERLINGER

Designed by

STEPHEN SCHMIDT

ST. MARTIN'S PRESS
NEW YORK

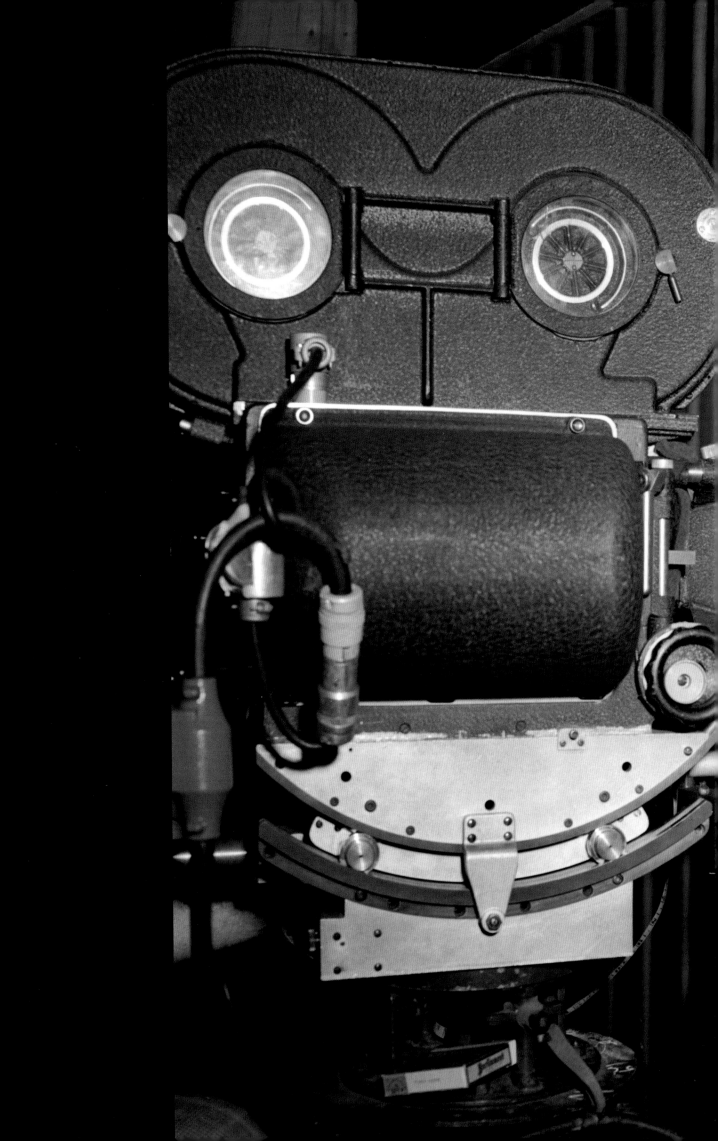

INTRODUCTION

Film history is filled with stars created by the studio system. Carefully controlled, modified, costumed, and trained, these performers often became much more than originally met the eye. Many had natural talent, some only charisma, and others great beauty. Occasionally, however, a performer emerged who, against all preconceived odds of what a star should be or look like, knocked down the walls of convention by becoming nothing other than what they already were. Frank Sinatra was the embodiment of this fundamental truth.

An entertainer who acted, an actor who produced, and finally a producer who also happened to be a world-famous singer, Sinatra proved to be a roulette wheel of constantly spinning talent, the likes of which Hollywood rarely matched on its own. His was a singular talent so profound that for decades when faced with changing times and attitudes, Sinatra effortlessly reinvented himself to fit the new ideas of cool.

Sinatra, instantly identifiable by just his last name, is the definition of a true star: a person who possesses the elusive qualities of innate likeability, charisma, talent, and personal magnetism.

Rarely, if ever, stopping to savor success, Sinatra bulldozed a career like no one else's. The legacy of his warp-speed life, work, and leisure stand apart from many of his contemporaries, who were essentially fulfilling a highly specialized audience expectation, blown up and out for the big screen. Most of the great stars in cinematic history—like Cary Grant, Marilyn Monroe, John Wayne, Bette Davis, or Charlie Chaplin—based their performances on an extension of a core character type. The downside to this was often typecasting. Sinatra, however, was able to take his signature persona and translate it successfully into many film genres—first as the comedic song-and-dance man, then as the dramatic actor and romantic lead, and finally as the tough guy and action hero. He could do anything.

Sinatra also respectfully challenged contemporary ideals of acting technique. While being humble enough to learn from his peers, he kept his acting style fresh and instinctual, and earned an Oscar at a time when many actors were either classically trained or coached in the "Method."

Sinatra, the smooth crooner, had an unhurried and meticulous way with a song. But as a movie star, he was in constant motion, an impatient actor in for a single take, maybe two. During the filming of *Ocean's 11* in 1960, Peter Lawford recalled, "I remember once the soundman kept complaining about an unusual number of low-flying airplanes which he was picking up through his earphones, and which were consequently being heard on the track. Well, after about the fourth take, which was unheard of for Frank, he said, 'Aw, f. . . it! Everyone knows they're airplanes!' Indeed! But flying through a bathroom?" Despite the production being his project, his party, Sinatra couldn't take the wait, having already moved past the scene in his mind. Moviemaking was a snail-paced process; Frank was rapid-fire, at his best when everyone else was just getting started.

Golden Boy

In 1941, on the assumption that the young singer might generate box office numbers to match record sales and concert grosses, Paramount propped Sinatra in front of the Tommy Dorsey Orchestra to sing "I'll Never Smile Again" in *Las Vegas Nights*. MGM followed suit the next year with the song "Moonlight Bay" in *Ship Ahoy*, no acting required. *Reveille with Beverly* (1943) at RKO featured a performance of "Night and Day," about which the film's star, Ann Miller, recalled, "A record would start to spin, then the camera would pan onto the record while the voice came on, and then to Frank's face with a big band backing him. Even way back then he was great, his voice sent tingles up your spine."

That same year the singer spoke his first lines on screen, "Good morning, I'm Frank Sinatra," and played a version of himself in *Higher and Higher*. Crooning a few new songs selected just for him, he invited comparisons to Bing Crosby, his own idol, and received encouraging press about his screen potential. Physically, he had unlikely prospects for movie stardom, but he was interestingly photogenic, with sharp cheekbones and large eyes to accompany "The Voice."

A musicalization of the Marx Brothers' *Room Service*, titled *Step Lively*, was released in 1944. Show business was again the background, and this time Frank played a character other than himself, a playwright named Glenn Russell. Sinatra was introduced to songwriters Sammy Cahn and Jule Styne, landed his first screen kiss (with Gloria DeHaven), and received top billing, a status that would come and go through the next decade.

Next up for Sinatra was joining the Navy—the MGM Navy—for *Anchors Aweigh* (1945), which paired the best singer with the best dancer as two sailors on a four-day pass in Hollywood. Gene Kelly took on the task of putting Sinatra on his dancing feet, and very nearly succeeded. Sinatra, as wide-eyed puppy dog Clarence Doolittle, struggles to keep up with his buddy/idol, the wolfish Joe Brady, in lady-killing and toe-tapping, but sings "I Fall in Love Too Easily" to a Best Song Oscar nomination. Kathryn Grayson as Susan captures Clarence's affections; she falls for Joe, and Clarence ultimately hooks up with Pamela Britton, the girl from hometown Brooklyn. The story is so lightweight it could be done in by the slightest sea breeze, but Sinatra is endearing, continually adjusting the angle of his sailor cap to match Joe's. There was some on-set trouble when Sinatra was vocal about his frustration with the sit-around-and-wait of moviemaking, as reported by columnist Louella Parsons, but his cast mates pledged their support to counter any future complaints.

MGM then placed Sinatra in a 1946 fictionalized movie portrait of composer Jerome Kern. Draped in a white tuxedo and backed by a white-wardrobed full orchestra, Sinatra performs "Ol' Man River" on a cavernous whitewashed set for the finale of *Till the Clouds Roll By*. The production number struck many wrong notes and was called into question by critics, and perhaps by Sinatra himself.

A modest black-and-white musical followed in 1947, *It Happened in Brooklyn*. A much more assured screen actor this time out, Sinatra plays Danny Miller, an aspiring singer returning from service in WWII. He is first paired with Kathryn Grayson, but is supplanted in her affections by Peter Lawford in what is essentially a replay of the *Anchors Aweigh* plot, Frank being left this time with his wartime memories of military nurse Gloria Grahame. Good reviews and good will resulted from this project, as Lawford noted that Frank was ". . . a joy to work with, which surprised everyone from the prop man to L. B. Mayer, because of his reputation, which preceded him, of his being difficult to get along with." A flash-forward of sorts to *On the Town* occurred in the picture when Sinatra's rendition of "Time After Time" was shot on location at the Brooklyn Bridge.

More than a few years later the Sinatra/Kelly chemistry was rekindled for a second effort, *Take Me Out to the Ball Game* (1949). Gene and Frank are a vaudeville song-and-dance team that moonlights as two-thirds of a baseball team's triple-play kings, along with Jules Munshin. Confident Kelly pursues Esther Williams, the owner of the team, while Betty Garrett literally shoulders slender Frank. The songs are not up MGM par, but Sinatra concentrated on improving his dance chops with Kelly's athletic oversight, and taking his turn as a real funny man, as if to make sure there would be a third act for this dream team.

And, of course, there was. Straight from *Ball Game* the boys were hustled into sailor suits once more for *On the Town*, Munshin as well. For twenty-four hours only, the three hit Manhattan in search of sights to see and love to make, "New York, New York" being "a wonderful town" (on Broadway it was allowed to be "a helluva town").

The movie is stage-bound for much of its running time, but benefits enormously from its opening and closing sequences shot in open air on location, which, in the era of studio back lots, was a minor revolution. Kelly once more scores the beautiful girl while Sinatra, as the anxious, orderly Chip, submits to the secondary romance with Betty Garrett, an aggressive cab driver. Sinatra was again coached through his dance numbers by Kelly (who also co-directed with Stanley Donen), and was by now a decent triple threat.

Just before the exuberant success of *On the Town*, two misbegotten productions seemed to dovetail with the maturing and shrinking of Sinatra's young fan-base. *The Kissing Bandit* and *The Miracle of the Bells* (both 1948), gave the distinct impression that his movie career had derailed, studio chiefs aiding in the decline. Sinatra was miscast in both films and looks uncomfortable, as if he is wishing them over and done. *Bandit* places him opposite Kathryn Grayson for a third tepid go-round, while *Miracle* tries hopelessly to fashion him into a priest, all efforts tedious and wasteful.

Double Dynamite (1951) was unfortunately a bomb without a fuse. In this RKO romantic caper with a song or two, slender and edgy Sinatra was mismatched with the curvy calm of Jane Russell. Groucho Marx had a bit of advice for his often-late costar, "I believe in being on time to work. The next time you show up late, you'd better be prepared to act for two, because I won't be here." A chastened Sinatra then paid strict attention to the daily roster, at least while Groucho was around.

Moving over to Universal, Sinatra made *Meet Danny Wilson* (1952), a show-biz tale told in noirish mode of a charming, brash singer, a hotheaded talent in too deep with a nightclub owner/racketeer and stuck on songbird Shelley Winters. Sinatra and Winters conjured no screen chemistry but plenty of on-set animosity as Sinatra insisted on making quick work of every scene. Caught during a downturn in his fame, Sinatra seems to be overcompensating, and slightly overplays the role. However, a definitive performance of "That Old Black Magic" is reviewed as being worth the price of the ticket.

Nevertheless, Sinatra's career as a motion picture star seemed a fizzle just as his rocket was about to launch. But an important project was in the works and he was sure there was a part he must go after: a coveted dramatic role in a prestige picture.

Dramatic Turns

Urgently seeking an audition for a pivotal role in *From Here to Eternity* (1953), Sinatra signed more than a few pleas—to Columbia studio head Harry Cohn—with his would-be alter ego's name, "Angelo Maggio." Sinatra's age, however, was a drawback. At thirty-eight he was considered too old for the part of the scrappy GI, and his crooner status stamped him as a lightweight actor. But his eventual audition impressed director Fred Zinnemann, and his agreement to a low paycheck impressed Cohn. The part was his.

Almost all of Maggio's scenes are duets with Prewitt, the lead role played by Montgomery Clift, the lauded actor who employed the "Method." This acting technique grew out of the rigorous Stanislavski system in Moscow, imported to New York by Lee Strasberg, Stella Adler, Elia Kazan, and others via the work of the Group Theatre and later, the Actors Studio. The Method was espoused in Hollywood through the classes of Michael Chekhov (nephew of playwright Anton), who was prominent in the Moscow Art Theatre. Clift, Marlon Brando, and James Dean boldly carried the flag of Method acting in film, making use of controversial techniques like sense memory and affective memory to connect to a character through personal emotion. Sinatra had his own non-method: a completely instinctual, spontaneous approach.

Sinatra, referred to often as "One-Take Charlie," was anything but a Method actor. Yet he was wise enough to recognize Clift as the finest actor with whom he had ever been paired, and decided to absorb some of what Clift brought to the set each day; he would need to add emotional musculature to his work just as Gene Kelly had required of him new physical muscles to learn to dance. Sinatra and Clift became good friends in much the same way Maggio and Prewitt bonded in the film.

The results were unanimously praised. Both actors received Oscar nominations, Sinatra taking home the gold statuette on one the biggest nights of his life, which he downplayed, but privately savored as the comeback he'd been envisioning.

After *From Here to Eternity* was released and Sinatra's storied comeback was officially underway, a minor film noir flooded with daylight offered an opportunity to further establish some serious acting credentials. John Baron, a high-strung, malicious assassin for hire, has his rifle trained on the president of the United States in *Suddenly* (1954).

The movie is a taut 75-minute thriller, heavy on the melodrama and tough-guy talk, which Sinatra rises above. As in *Eternity*, the character is killed, but here it's a release rather than a tragedy. The movie's premise forced a reexamination after the events of November 1963, when Sinatra felt compelled to use his influence to have *Suddenly* pulled permanently from broadcast television.

Not as a Stranger, directed by Stanley Kramer for release in 1955, cast 40-year-old Sinatra as med student Alfred Boone, third-billed to Robert Mitchum and Olivia de Havilland. In this soapy hospital drama, Sinatra provides some comic relief, stealing scenes and arguably the picture as well.

A card dealer, a drug addict, and a would-be drummer make up the parts of the sum that is *The Man With the Golden Arm*—the triple-entendre title of the 1955 movie Sinatra chose to continue his run as a serious actor. With an Oscar on his mantel, Sinatra had only to add some personal research to his arsenal, something he had rarely, if ever, done.

Against standard practice, he was permitted to observe a young heroin addict in the midst of withdrawal at a rehabilitation facility. Quite shaken and feeling he did not wish to see more, Sinatra felt suitably "armed" with the compassion to play, and behavior to authenticate, the role in which he was so interested. Hollywood legend has it that Sinatra far surpassed director Otto Preminger's expectations for the detox scene, nailing it in one take.

Sinatra and Preminger, each having a combative nature and dark reputation, were forecast to combust on a daily basis. In fact, they got along quite well, teaming up to assist the insecure Kim Novak through some difficult scene-work.

Preminger brought other invaluable collaborators on board: Saul Bass, who designed the spare, pulsing title sequence, and Elmer Bernstein, who composed the jazz score, all rumble and dissonance. The jazz sequences were recorded by Shorty Rogers and His Giants, with percussionist Shelly Manne, who coached Sinatra on the drums.

On a bus returning him from rehab, Sinatra as Frankie Machine steps down into a bottomed-out streetscape meant to suggest, but not mimic, an urban but small-time ghetto of no return. Preminger, having been a student of the influential stage director and impresario Max Reinhardt in Vienna, kept the setting conceptual—cramped, claustrophobic, devoid of realist detail. In the film's first minute, Frankie pauses before the ironically capsule-shaped bar window, gazing inside, seeing old friends and enablers. The camera moves through the door and swivels to face Frankie, who breaks the cinematic "fourth wall" by looking directly into the camera lens, just for an instant, as if there were a story he knows but has yet to experience, personally challenging the audience and inviting them to witness this cautionary fable.

Sinatra's newfound dedication and daring portrayal were rewarded with a Best

Actor nomination, but the Oscar was lost to his *Eternity* nemesis, Ernest Borgnine, for *Marty*. On more than one occasion Sinatra wondered aloud, given his rave reviews and personal commitment to his role, if he had actually won the award for the wrong picture.

Sinatra chose a western as his initial foray into producing, placing himself in the title role of *Johnny Concho* (1956). The cowardly Concho goes after revenge and redemption against the gunslingers who murdered his brother. Phyllis Kirk replaced the initially cast Gloria Vanderbilt in the subplot romance. Reviews for Sinatra were decent but not enthusiastic; the movie itself was panned and failed at the box office.

A biopic, *The Joker Is Wild*, next benefited from Sinatra's multiple talents when he bought the rights to the true story of show business legend Joe E. Lewis, a cocky nightclub singer mixed up in Roaring Twenties gangland rivalries. As payback for disloyalty, his vocal cords are slashed and Lewis makes his tortured, alcoholic way back by reinventing himself as a club comedian, three dames lending comfort through the turmoil. Here Sinatra played an antihero before the concept had a designation, and poured much of himself into his multidimensional portrayal. The success of *The Joker Is Wild* included an Academy Award: Best Original Song to Jimmy Van Heusen and Sammy Cahn, who wrote "All the Way" for the film and for Sinatra.

Shirley MacLaine had a lot to be hopeful and thankful for when Sinatra selected her as the good-natured girl-for-hire Ginny in the cast of *Some Came Running* (1958). Dean Martin had already placed himself directly in Sinatra's field of vision at a party, as a result landing the role of the gambler Bama. The trio, soon great pals, accompanied director Vincente Minnelli to Madison, Indiana, for the long location shoot. To survive the small-town quiet and confinement, Sinatra invited Dean to join him in nightly revels after the day's work was done, with Shirley essentially keeping house for the drinking, card-playing duo, an arrangement that mirrored the film's story.

In the midst of delivering a fine performance as Dave Hirsh, a WWII vet returning home after his Army discharge to write, Sinatra was feeling anxious and impatient with Minnelli's careful, no-detail-too-small-or-large style. He not only voiced his displeasure but took the step of chartering a plane, rustling up Dean, and flying back to L.A. well before shooting was completed, returning only when he felt his point had been made. The movie and the role are placed high on Sinatra's critical list, but the overt accolades went to MacLaine. At Sinatra's insistence, the picture's ending was rewritten to have Ginny shield Dave from a fatal bullet, thus, in Sinatra's real-life scenario, assuring Maclaine of an Oscar nomination. It played out just like that.

Broadway Mellow-dy

Riding the wave of a refreshed career in recordings and movies by the mid-1950s, Sinatra joined Doris Day in *Young at Heart*, a remake of *Four Daughters* (1938). In the John Garfield part, here named Barney Sloan, Sinatra is a pianist/arranger for a composer. He slumps, smokes, dons the fedora that will become a personal logo, and brings the movie to a climax with a suicide attempt. Yet, he sensitively sings "One for My Baby" and the title tune, and duets with Doris on "You, My Love." The attractive teaming of Sinatra and Day was a solid hit for Warner Bros. in 1954, and was the last time Sinatra would play the gifted outsider in a small-scale show business fable with music.

Sinatra then let it be known: He was the obvious and only choice for the role of gambler Sky Masterson in *Guys and Dolls*, the part zoot-suiting him perfectly. He was resentful when it was handed to Marlon Brando. Sinatra had to settle for Nathan Detroit, crap game proprietor and perpetual fiancé to showgirl Miss Adelaide. The instant Broadway classic by Frank Loesser, by way of the Times Square tales of Damon Runyon, was destined to be one of the big movie hits of 1955. Sinatra nursed his grudge throughout production, every opportunity taken to refer to Brando as "Mumbles." The ill will seemed to limit his performance. Even as he expertly sings the title song, he wished instead to be performing "Luck Be a Lady," which went to Brando. The director Joe Mankiewicz, despite the masterful *All About Eve* on his résumé, contrived a strange hybrid, delivering to critics an uninspired un-musical that nevertheless was a box office hit.

High Society (1956) was not Broadway-born, but had a potent Broadway pedigree with *The Philadelphia Story* as its source and Cole Porter tunes to make it sing. Sinatra seems an unpromising counterpart to James Stewart as journalist Mike Connor. Even more unlikely is Bing Crosby (age fifty-three) in the Cary Grant role as the ex-husband of Tracy Lord, aka Katharine Hepburn, here played by Grace Kelly (age twenty-six). Sinatra, however, was eager to play opposite Crosby, the idol of his adolescence, and Grace, the aristocratic beauty. All are charming, but the extra wit and zip necessary to make this an entertainment classic are missing. Everyone apparently had a nice time working together, but after Louis Armstrong jazzes up the proceedings, his absence is palpable. A situation full of irony came about when a duet by Bing and Grace, the ballad "True Love," sold in platinum-record numbers while Sinatra scored no hits at all from the movie. And Grace Kelly had never sung on camera before.

Moving over from MGM to Columbia in 1957 for *Pal Joey* provided Sinatra with a signature characterization: the singing, swinging, can't pin-me-down, eternal bachelor opportunist Joey Evans. The Broadway Joey was a dancer, but this crooning Joey is much more on target with its cynical balladeer on the make for the heiress Vera (Rita Hayworth) and exotic dancer Linda (Kim Novak). With classic Rodgers and Hart songs on tap, Sinatra immortalizes his hip, cool, snappy man-about-town, a lovable cad, coat draped over one shoulder, fedora angled, always on his way out the door. A perfect fit, the role won him a Golden Globe Award. Yet he was 42, and it was not a very good year—Sinatra was suing *Look* magazine, good friend Humphrey Bogart passed away, and his television variety show failed.

In 1959, Sinatra was again on a soundstage, this time at Twentieth Century–Fox, for a Broadway-to-Hollywood makeover, *Can-Can*, with a score by Cole Porter and again costarring Shirley MacLaine. The company was in the middle of production when Russian Premier Nikita Khrushchev and his entourage visited Los Angeles. A gala luncheon was hastily arranged, hosted by Sinatra, with four hundred of the Hollywood elite in attendance, after which the premier and his wife were treated to an energetic performance of the French revue dance, the movie's centerpiece. Amid flashing petticoats, girls in flying splits, and bloomers unveiled,

Khrushchev feigned outrage. The presentation was swarmed by national and international press, and featured in both *Look* and *Life*. However, that was as good as it got for *Can-Can*. That publicity far outsold the finished product; it was a dance film whose male star didn't dance a step, sang too few songs, and whose badly conceived wardrobe was far more ring-a-ding than period-perfect.

The Color Orange

The long first scene, essentially Act One, of *The Tender Trap* (1955) is a bliss of mid-century Hollywood modern. This dream of a bachelor pad, all low-slung levels backed by a spectacular floor-to-ceiling view of the Brooklyn Bridge, is accented in delicious shades of peach, tangerine, and orange, as if Frank Sinatra himself had thrown the pillows. His daughter Tina pointed out before Sinatra's passing, "My father is very sensitive to light and shadow and color. To him, colors enhance life. He loves bright colors. Orange is his favorite...."

The stage was thus set for a swinging, martini-clinking bachelor in 1950s paradise, in this case Charlie Reader, a Manhattan theatrical agent. He has a woman (Celeste Holm), among many, an envious best friend (David Wayne), and a charming new client (the very young Debbie Reynolds), who subconsciously primes her "tender trap." Director Charles Walters found himself with highly musical actors and a mandate to film this straight comedy in CinemaScope. He would take advantage of his cast and justify the widescreen format by shooting Sinatra alone from an extreme distance in a pre-credits sequence. Earth and sky bisecting the frame, Sinatra sings the title tune as he and the camera approach one another. The other three join him for a reprise of the number at the close, bookending the story. Sinatra performs just the one song, and adeptly demonstrates his appealing skills as a comic actor.

United Artists had "high hopes" for another free-wheeling bachelor comedy starring, as *Playboy* magazine put it, "sex idol" Sinatra. Set in citrus-colored and sunlit Miami and directed in 1959 by Frank Capra, *A Hole in the Head* presents Sinatra as Tony Manetta, a comic dreamer, a fantasy risk-taker, but also the father of a pre-teen son. Tony squares off against his older brother, played by Edward G.

Robinson, over the fate of the boy, Ally, the conflict echoed on-set as Sinatra and Robinson locked horns over rehearsals and multiple takes.

Sinatra impressed audiences once more with his relaxed comedy rhythms, and charted a big pop hit with "High Hopes," which won the Oscar for writers Cahn and Van Heusen. With newly minted lyrics, the song helped position Jack Kennedy as the front-runner for president in 1960.

Sinatra further confirmed the public's perception of him by turning Neil Simon's *Come Blow Your Horn* into a swinging Sinatra vehicle in 1963. Big-time NYC bachelor Alan Baker, hi-fi in the background, cocktail in hand, serially seduces Connie, Peggy, and Mrs. Eckman (Barbara Rush, Jill St. John, and Phyllis McGuire). Alan's younger brother Buddy (Tony Bill) wants in on the life and the style, setting up a domestic crisis with their parents. Sinatra cruises through his part, commanding the proceedings while wearing an alpaca sweater in his favored orange.

The antithesis of all that swinging and girl-chasing came in 1965 with *Marriage on the Rocks*. As though to prove he could—and/or as a nod to advancing age—Sinatra signed on to play advertising executive Dan Edwards, a very settled suburban husband and father. To maintain Sinatra's comfort level, Dean Martin appears as best friend Ernie, and to add a bit of class, Deborah Kerr plays Valerie, the bored, unsatisfied wife. Nancy Jr. steps in for a delightful turn as daughter Tracy. Unmarital but not hilarious adventures ensue, and the picture is unfortunately not worthy of the talent involved. The high jinks on set may have been more entertaining, as Sinatra and Martin christened the statuesque Deborah "The Jolly Green Giant" when she was costumed in jade-toned chiffon.

Clansville

It would be a gas! Show up at the Sands Hotel in Vegas. Shoot a caper flick all afternoon with a loose script. Do two shows a night in the Copa Room with no script at all. Drinks, chicks, bed at four, maybe five. A few winks till noon. Rinse and repeat....

That was the formula for a lot of fun, some bucks, and a big box-office hit in 1960, when Sinatra gathered the Rat Pack for his preferred subtitle for the project,

"The Summit at the Sands." Dean Martin, Sammy Davis, Jr., Peter Lawford, Joey Bishop, Angie Dickinson—"the innest in-group in the world," as *Playboy* called them—took a gamble on *Ocean's 11*. At his most relaxed and self-assured, Sinatra as Danny Ocean schemes with his ten buddies to hit five casinos simultaneously on New Year's Eve, without guns, without experience. This is almost slice-of-life Sinatra, as he takes charge of the heist and the show.

"Pocket handkerchiefs are optional, but I always wear one, usually orange." This is Sinatra's advice for black-tie dressing, on display nightly at the Sands during the *Ocean's* location shoot. Personal wardrobe was always an essential consideration for Sinatra, especially during the Clan/Rat Pack years. Highly polished shoes, the right hat at a rakish angle, cuff links but no other jewelry—these were hallmarks of his sixties style. Robert Wagner adds, "For a long time Frank liked his suits to be made by Sy Devore....Sy loved shine—rayons and mohairs and shark skins. At some point in the sixties Frank had 150 suits...." The Pack followed his lead, Dean Martin in particular, until Devore haberdashery filled the wardrobe trailer for *Ocean's 11*.

The tag line could have read "The Summit Goes West" for the 1962 remake of *Gunga Din*, retitled *Sergeants 3*, with Sinatra reuniting with Sammy Davis, Jr., Dean Martin, and The Clan. Native Americans, a massacre, a town called Medicine Bend, the U.S. cavalry, and Lawford and Bishop all mixed it up for a mildly funny comic western. Sinatra's M.O., to have great fun with friends, and by the way, make a movie, resulted in some seat-of-the-pants filming. "It was all so nuts," Sammy Davis, Jr., remembered. Sinatra "was told, 'This movie is too long.' So Frank grabbed the script and pulled out a fistful of pages and tore them up. 'There,' he said. 'It's shorter now.'"

4 for Texas (1963) quickly brought back Frank and Dean as Zach Thomas and Joe Jarrett in a business/romantic rivalry set in Galveston, for which Ursula Andress and Anita Ekberg lent bosomy support. As Sinatra was often on the outs with director/screenwriter Robert Aldrich, the best lines were given to Martin, and more screen time as well.

A musical version by Cahn and Van Heusen of the Robin Hood legend, transported to gangland Chicago in the Roaring Twenties, was proposed, and Frank was in, with Sammy and Dean backing him up, for *Robin and the 7 Hoods* (1964). Also joining this musical mob were Bing Crosby, Peter Falk, and Barbara Rush. Principal photography began in late 1963, but was briefly and abruptly halted by the assassination of President Kennedy in November, and Frank Jr.'s kidnapping two weeks later. The dire events delayed but did not stall the production; Falk and Davis made lively, even endearing gangsters, and Sinatra had the occasion to sing "My Kind of Town," and hoof a little with Bing and Dean.

But the times they were a-changin'. Six weeks after the opening of *7 Hoods*, *A Hard Day's Night* was released, and The Beatles ushered in a new brand of musical and cinematic cool for the sixties.

A Man in a Uniform

Frank Sinatra may have been prevented from serving in the military during World War II, but he "served his country" on screen over and over. Sinatra played a soldier in extremis (*From Here to Eternity*), and in combat beyond the battlefield (*Kings Go Forth, None But the Brave*). He was a post-war vet, returning home (*Some Came Running*), on to new endeavors benign (*It Happened in Brooklyn*), or nefarious (*Ocean's 11, Assault on a Queen*), or undercover (*The Naked Runner*), or a warrior mentally damaged (*Suddenly, The Manchurian Candidate*). And then, of course, there were the singing, dancing sailors in *Anchors Aweigh* and *On the Town*.

Costuming Sinatra in period clothing was always a problem; his was a thoroughly contemporary persona. So no one should have been surprised at the outcome of *The Pride and the Passion*, in 1957, when he took on a role that fit him as poorly as the black wig and ragged peasant uniform required to play it. In addition to Sinatra, Stanley Kramer enlisted Cary Grant, Sophia Loren (in her English language debut), and thousands of Spanish locals to tell the epic story of a massive, abandoned seven-ton cannon laboriously maneuvered to gain advantage against the invading army of Napoleon in 1810 Spain. Producer/Director Kramer agreed to shooting Sinatra's scenes first, explaining, "[He] is a tremendously talented man, intuitive and fast, which is good for him but not always good for the other actors. . . . He didn't want to rehearse. . . . or wait around while the crowd scenes were being set up." Once his scenes were in the can, Sinatra hastily retreated back to L.A., awaiting the company's return to complete the film on sound stages and the backlot.

Sinatra did double-duty on *Never So Few* (1959) as star and producer. A Pacific Theater WWII story told with location shooting in Burma, Ceylon, and Thailand, the film places Sinatra, as Col. Tom Reynolds, opposite Italian bombshell Gina Lollobrigida and in action with Peter Lawford, Charles Bronson, and Steve McQueen, a television star Sinatra promoted to the movie forefront. Sinatra turned in a respectable performance, both on and off-screen.

Almost immediately after *Ocean's 11*, Sinatra indulged in a little more criminality via the single-named Harry in *The Devil at 4 O'Clock* (1961). Together with Spencer Tracy as the unpriestly Father Matthew Doonan, Sinatra's dangerous convict rises to the occasion when an erupting volcano threatens leper colony children at a school on the South Pacific island of Talua, ground zero for serial disasters of biblical character and size, complete with a heavenly chorus. Sinatra felt privileged to be sharing the screen with the revered Tracy, but still subverted the location shooting schedule in Hawaii with his island-to-island campaigning for JFK in a chartered plane.

Army Major Bennett Marco has been eerily "washed and dry-cleaned" by North Korean communists as *The Manchurian Candidate* begins. The 1962 film, skillfully and intelligently put together by director John Frankenheimer and his collaborators, became the high point of Sinatra's career in motion pictures. Marco's—and his fellow soldiers'—bizarre nightmares cue the puzzle-piece psychological thriller that has something to say about conspiracy, power, madness, and covert wars in peacetime, the Cuban Missile Crisis having eerily played out not long before the film's release.

The assassination plot resonated with Sinatra, who had portrayed a would-be assassin less than a decade before in *Suddenly*. He must have pondered the origins, the stakes, the consequences of such dire actions, his worst fears realized in November 1963 when the Dallas tragedy took place. Following Kennedy's death, Sinatra felt personally responsible to make the films unavailable to the general public. *Suddenly* simply disappeared; *The Manchurian Candidate* became for a time a lost classic.

In this now reclaimed masterpiece, with stellar support from Angela Lansbury, Laurence Harvey, Janet Leigh, and Henry Silva, Sinatra counters his "swinging cool" image, hand-tooling a performance ticking with tension and fevered fatigue, in a picture for which edgy superlatives are not sufficient. Sinatra was immensely proud and humble, in turn, about his contribution.

He revisited the Second World War for *Von Ryan's Express* in 1965, first set in a German POW camp in Italy, then on a commandeered troop train chugging through the countryside. The role of Lt. Col. Joseph Ryan was a good fit for Sinatra, since as his lines were abbreviated and the action sequences did not necessarily require his immediate presence. Suspenseful, but also punctuated with comedic moments, the movie succeeds despite some rough cutting and awkward staging. Sinatra, as a producer, had the feel-good ending revised, adding shock and substance to the climax in which Ryan is gunned down before he can rejoin the moving train after a successful showdown with the advancing Nazi forces.

A Rod Serling screenplay lured Sinatra back to double-tasking as producer/star. *Assault on a Queen* (1966) cast him as ex-submarine officer Mark Brittain, now the owner of a charter boat business. A deep-sea treasure hunt develops into a major heist involving a sunken German sub, $1,000,000 in gold, and the *Queen Mary*. New star Virna Lisi appears as an additional golden enticement and the movie features some nice chemistry between Lisi's treasure hunter and Sinatra's sea captain.

John Wayne had a project in mind about the Israeli War of Independence, which would become *Cast a Giant Shadow* (1966), that he pitched to Kirk Douglas. Wayne and Douglas would take the lead roles, supported by an all-star cast. "We got Sinatra to play a small part [Vince, a pilot]," Douglas remembered, also mentioning Yul Brynner, Angie Dickinson, and Senta Berger. "As a matter of fact, there were too many stars in it. It took away from the significance of the piece." The overloaded epic came to be known as "Cast a Giant Shudder."

Law and Disorder

In *The Naked Runner* (1967), Sam Laker, a former WWII officer/marksman and now a businessman in London, is recruited to assassinate (the word and the deed arise again) a freed political prisoner before the Kremlin can probe his secrets. Sinatra's Sam is a man in too deep in Cold War fallout, with the life of his son being used as leverage to force his hand. The movie, chasing some then-fashionable James Bondian cool, failed to impress, but Sinatra's mature control in espionage-land was praised. However, Sinatra was not taken with swinging London, hurrying his director and crew and managing an early escape.

Back on familiar turf in Miami, USA, for *Tony Rome* (1967), Sinatra plays a private detective with police and underworld connections, living out of his boat, driving a convertible heap, but still attracting the ladies (Jill St. John, Gena Rowlands, Sue Lyon). A simple favor for a paying client sends Rome down a slippery rabbit hole of kidnapping, blackmail, and murder. Many guns, several dead bodies, a lot of lies and secrets, and a few invitations to bed later, Rome drives off alone, the convoluted case another done deal. A semi-prototype for some TV detectives to come, the movie was received politely. Sinatra, however, scored points for playing his age with a certain amount of rumpled, hard-edged grace. The fedora got good reviews as well.

The Detective (1968) was Sinatra's dip into the style of seamy, gritty, adult realism that was reshaping American cinema in the late 1960s. Det. Joe Leland, NYPD, is double-tracking a wealthy gay man's brutal murder amid allegations of corruption involving politicians, developers, and the police. Lee Remick plays his wife, Karen, while other roles are filled by exciting newcomers Jacqueline Bisset and Al Freeman, Jr., young character actor Robert Duvall, and old character actor Jack Klugman. Sinatra bears the brunt of the shocking subject matter, speaking the raw dialogue (perhaps mainstream cinema's first mention of the words "penis" and "semen"), while, as he said, "...always trying to keep a little tenderness in it somewhere."

Tony Rome played a return engagement in 1968. *Lady in Cement* is a more comedic take on the Miami P.I., the plot focusing at first on the discovery of a corpse—a woman, her feet in concrete, found off the coast by scuba divers. The heiress Kit Forrest (Raquel Welch) may or may not be a suspect, but her spectacular body is thoroughly investigated as the case continues. Richard Conte (a favorite Sinatra supporting actor), Dan Blocker, and Lainie Kazan show up to help or hinder. To stay put and stay interested, Sinatra booked a gig at the Fontainebleau Hotel showroom to coincide with the shooting schedule, lightening his mood and thus lending the refreshed Tony Rome a lot of casual throwaway style. In the end Tony gets the girl, and the movie an R rating (nudity/violence), a first for a Sinatra picture.

The comedy-western *Dirty Dingus Magee* became Sinatra's swan song in 1970, when he announced his first retirement. Sinatra saddles into the character Magee, a grizzled old grifter hoping for a last loot of gold, and a hightail across the border into the cartoon sunset. A talented cast without star names labored to elevate the material, but the critics and audiences wouldn't go along for the ride.

Sinatra came close to taking the Clint Eastwood role in *Dirty Harry* in 1971, but a wrist he broke while shooting *The Manchurian Candidate* ultimately took him out of the running. The accident left him unable to comfortably and convincingly handle the weighty Magnum pistol that would become an Eastwood signature weapon.

A made-for-TV movie, *Contract on Cherry Street*, in 1977, brought Sinatra back to New York as Frank Hovannes, a deputy police inspector investigating the Mob and its numbers-running. Hovannes turns vigilante when a close friend and colleague is killed in the street, and the bodies pile up from there, leaving the critics wondering what drew Sinatra to the violent material as his first dramatic foray into television.

After ten years away from the big screen, Sinatra agreed to return for a movie of one of Lawrence Sanders's series of crime novels, and the possibility of a film franchise with his name and fame attached. *The First Deadly Sin*, a 1980 release, again positioned Sinatra with the NYPD, this time as Edward X. Delaney, a soon-to-retire captain with a terminally ill wife, played by Faye Dunaway. An intriguing duo, Frank Sinatra and Faye Dunaway act their touching scenes in hospital hush, against the contrasting mayhem stalking the streets of the city. A serial murderer is viciously striking down his random victims with an ice axe. Graphic images of surgery and slaughter jump-start the story, while menacing hints of noir style counter the hopeful lights of the Christmas season. Sinatra expertly underplays, his face a tale of hard times.

Actively Engaged

One indelible conviction that informed Sinatra's life, from his first sung notes to his final bows, was his profound commitment to the cause of human equality. Racial, religious, and cultural exclusion and persecution hurt him personally, Sinatra having been brought up in a close Catholic family on the rough streets of Hoboken, New Jersey. Sammy Davis, Jr., paid tribute to his friend and colleague with these words, "During three decades, along all the highways of my youth, Frank has always been there for me." Sinatra was a champion of Sammy's prodigious talents well before the emergence of the gang of five, but casting him in three popular movies made an even broader, louder statement of embrace in the midst of the civil rights movement. Sammy and Frank were brothers, directly from the heart.

Back in 1945, with prompting from director Mervyn LeRoy and support from RKO, the young Sinatra literally lent his voice to the cause in a short film called *The House I Live In*. He sings a fervent anthem and speaks to a gang intent on harming the Jewish boy in their midst, declaring that a bully has no ground on which to stand, as "God didn't create one people better than another." An Oscar from the Academy of Motion Picture Arts and Sciences seconded the praise from the Hollywood community, or from its liberal contingent at least. Gene Kelly congratulated his friend: "I'm proud of you Frank, 'cause that short will make a big contribution to the cause of tolerance."

Kings Go Forth (1958) addressed American attitudes with a multi-genre fable: war story, melodrama, buddy picture. In WWII France, Sinatra and combat pal Tony Curtis both fall for Natalie Wood as a girl with a black father, her mother now a widow. The casting of the Caucasian Miss Wood in some ways represents a failure of nerve, an opportunity wasted, but a message was delivered, however blunted and blurred. Sinatra's army captain in *Never So Few* (1959) is compelled to speak up, to strongly object to a U.S. colonel's repeated prejudice: his lack of regard for the Native Americans ("Indians," at the time) under his command, and his disrespect of the indigenous culture and people of the country who were serving as his host and base of operations.

Sinatra's sole outing as a director, *None but the Brave*, in 1965, afforded him the chance to humanize a bygone American enemy. On an island in the South Pacific, the world war already over, American and Japanese combatants find common ground and community before the Japanese are all killed by a late-arriving U.S. destroyer. Only five Americans survived. Tatsuya Mihashi narrates the film in accented English, perhaps a first, while the Japanese soldiers speak their own language, subtitled, a strategy ahead of its time. The film concludes with a simple anti-war message: "Nobody wins."

"Tolerance is a theme that's close to his heart," says Sinatra's daughter Nancy, which tells us a great deal of what we need to know about her father. Sinatra the humanitarian was a lifelong determination, and he knew that a movie could be much more than an entertainment; it could be enlightenment.

Serving as enlightenment for more than just the moviegoing public during his lifetime, Sinatra's films have been remade and recast to much fanfare and financial success. However, as with all remakes, important details can often get lost in the retelling. For how can cultural landmarks so singular, identifiable, and unique as *The Manchurian Candidate* or *Ocean's 11* be matched? Glossed up for a new generation they looked great, but a copy is still a copy even with a new shiny cover.

Looking back at the man and his career, one can say with certainty that there will never be another Frank Sinatra. How could there be? A legend in his own lifetime and beyond, Sinatra stands at the pinnacle of success and fame, style and creation. A talent not only for his generation, but one for the ages.

David Wills
Los Angeles, 2015

"People often remark that I'm pretty lucky. Luck is only important in so far as getting the chance to sell yourself at the right moment. After that, you've got to have talent and know how to use it."

—Frank Sinatra

Signing autographs for the
fans, Los Angeles, 1943.
Photo by Gene Lester.

"The crooner certainly doesn't fulfill the cinema's traditional ideal of a romantic figure, which may be a break for him eventually. He... appears more at ease than we expected, and should find a place as a film personality with careful choice of subjects. Crosby did it, didn't he?"

—John L. Scott (*Los Angeles Times*, review, *Higher and Higher*, 1943)

OPPOSITE *Higher and Higher*, 1943. **ABOVE** With costars Marcy McGuire (left) and Michèle Morgan.

ABOVE Insert poster, *Step Lively*, 1944.
RIGHT As Glenn Russell, *Step Lively*.

"With the Sinatra Swoon & Squeal Society in force at the Palace Theater, where *Step Lively* is displaying their idol under favorable conditions, it is not always possible to pay attention to the picture. Sinatra himself, cast in the modest role of the young playwright whose money and play have been taken without compensation, is better than in his previous efforts. He looks better, acts better, and sings in the manner that made him famous. Apparently, The Voice is here to stay."

—Archer Winston (*New York Post*, review, *Step Lively*, 1944)

OPPOSITE AND ABOVE 1943.

"I couldn't walk, let alone dance. I was a guy who got up and hung on to a microphone....And one of the reasons I became a 'star' was Gene Kelly."

—Frank Sinatra

CROONER CLOSE-UP.....When The Voice really gets under way his expressions range from tender abstraction to primitive passion. During his rendition of "What Makes the Sunset" in his current Metro-Goldwyn-Mayer Technicolor musical, "Anchors Aweigh," the candid camera caught the crooner in close-up. Results are shown in the following pictures. Gene Kelly, Kathryn Grayson are starred with Sinatra in the film, which was directed by George Sidney and produced by Joe Pasternak.

A dreamy passage gives him an out-of-this-world look.

1333x44,40

"I ventured down to Times Square and was literally scared away. The police estimated that 10,000 kids were queued up six abreast…and another 20,000 were running wild in Times Square….Girls shreiked, fainted—or swooned—fell down, were stepped on and pulled up by their companions and resumed screaming. They rushed the ticket booth and damaged it. Windows were broken."

—Earl Wilson (reporting on the opening day of *Anchors Aweigh*, New York, October 1945)

LEFT As Clarence Doolittle, *Anchors Aweigh*, 1945.
ABOVE With costar Gene Kelly.

"God didn't create one people better than another. Your blood is the same as mine, and mine is the same as his. You know what this country is? It's made up of a hundred different kinds of people—and they're all Americans. . . . Let's use our good American brains and not fight each other."

—Frank Sinatra (from *The House I Live In*, 1945)

ABOVE One-sheet poster, *The House I Live In*, 1945. **OPPOSITE** With George Murphy and Peggy Ann Garner, at the 18th Academy Awards, 1946. Sinatra accepted a special Oscar for *The House I Live In*.

MOVIE STARS PARADE

FEBRUARY

Super All-Star Birthday Number!

EXCLUSIVE—FRANK SINATRA'S NEW MOVIE IN STORY FORM!

A FAWCETT PUBLICATION

MOVIE STORY MAGAZINE

AUGUST

FRANK SINATRA AND GLORIA DE HAVEN

NEW PICTURES WITH GARY COOPER, INGRID BERGMAN, FRED MacMURRAY
BARBARA STANWYCK, EDDIE BRACKEN, ELLA RAINES, RED SKELTON

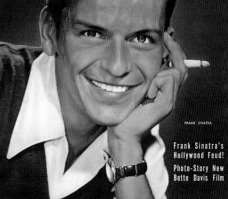

STARDOM

Hollywood's Most Exciting Magazine

15¢
MLA

December

FRANK SINATRA

Frank Sinatra's Hollywood Feud!

Photo-Story New Bette Davis Film

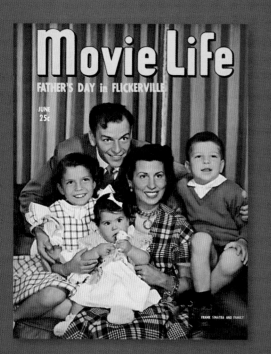

Movie Life

FATHER'S DAY in FLICKERVILLE

JUNE
25¢

FRANK SINATRA AND FAMILY

COMPLETE DATA ON 100 STARS — 40 SPECIAL PORTRAITS

SCREEN ALBUM

Frank Sinatra
Voice of America

Modern Screen

SEPTEMBER
15¢

DELL

SINATRA'S LIFE STORY!

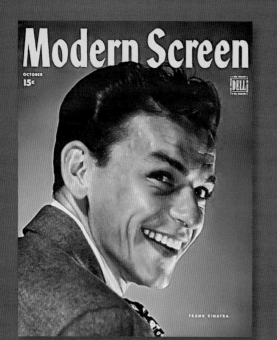

Modern Screen

OCTOBER
15¢

DELL

FRANK SINATRA

MOVIE STARS PARADE

DECEMBER
25¢
PBC

RADIO PARADE

BERGMAN · CALHOUN
LIZ TAYLOR
BOGART-BACALL
All in Color

FRANK SINATRA

Screen stories

DELL
15¢

JAN

GENE KELLY
VERA-ELLEN

3 GOBS and 3 GIRLS
"On the Town"

FRANK SINATRA
BETSY GARRETT
JULES MUNSHIN
ANN MILLER

Modern Screen

JANUARY 15c

DELL

FRANK SINATRA
MAN OF THE YEAR—(p. 28)

OPPOSITE Fan magazines, c. mid-1940s. **ABOVE** *Modern Screen*, January 1947.

41

"My idea with that song, was to have a… little fellow do it—somebody who made you believe he was tired of livin' and scared of dyin'. That's how you do it, Frankie."

—Jerome Kern (composer, "Ol' Man River," on Frank Sinatra's performance in *Till the Clouds Roll By*, 1946)

Performing "Ol' Man River," *Till the Clouds Roll By*, 1946.

OPPOSITE 1946. **ABOVE** 1945. Photo by Pagano.

IN THE PALM OF HIS HAND...Frank Sinatra holds the world...the gold globe presented to him by the Hollywood Foreign Correspondents Association in recognition of his efforts to promote racial tolerance. Before the cast of his latest Metro-Goldwyn-Mayer film, "It Happened in Brooklyn," including Kathryn Grayson, Peter Lawford, Lauritz Melchior and Jimmy Durante, Marina Cisternas, president of the Association, made the presentation at lunch in the M-G-M Commissary. Also present were Angela Lansbury, Hurd Hatfield, Marilyn Maxwell, Lina Romay and representatives of the correspondents who circle the globe with Hollywood news.
Left to right: Lauritz Melchior, Howard Hill, Peter Lawford, Frank Sinatra, Marina Cisternas, William Mooring, Hurd Hatfield, Michele Green and Nora Laing.

"Frank, of course, thrills the customers with his vocalizing, but it's his naturalness and easy-going charm that beget applause. It just seems like all of a sudden it's spring and Frankie is an actor. His comical duet with Durante provoked great whoops of approval from the boys and girls out front."

—Sara Hamilton (*Los Angeles Examiner*, review, *It Happened in Brooklyn,* 1947)

ABOVE Frank Sinatra receiving a special Golden Globe for "Promoting Good Will," 1947. OPPOSITE With costar Jimmy Durante, *It Happened in Brooklyn*, 1947.

A LESSON IN SONG....Frank Sinatra and Jimmy Durante join
voices for the year's most unusual duet. It's for Metro-
Goldwyn-Mayer's gay new musical film hit, "It Happened In
Brooklyn." The Nose shows The Voice how to put across a
song.   chnozzola and Frankie are pictured here swinging
it in typical Durante fashion. They also do a few fancy
dance steps. Cast of the new tunefest also boasts Kathryn
Grayson and Peter Lawford. Richard Whorf directed. Jack
Cummings produced.

4. Me foist, says Durante as Frankie takes the lead.
   1388-67

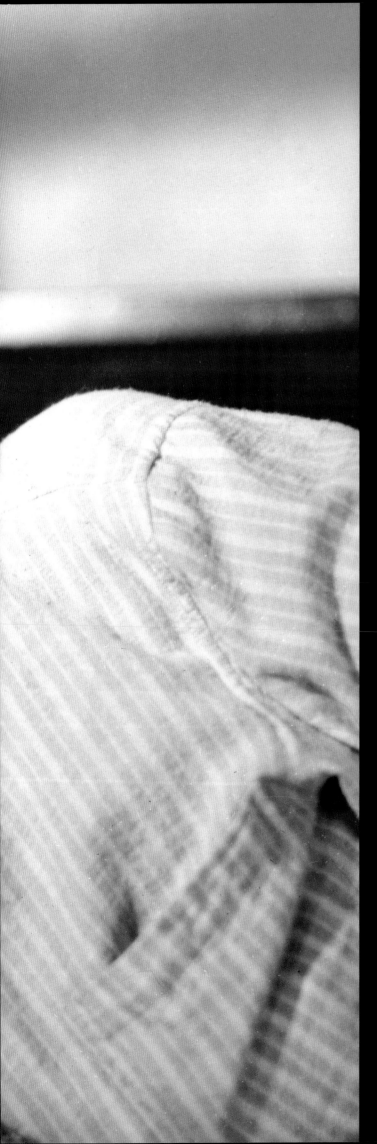

"Directing Frank is a revelation. He blends in more than you'd think with the other cast members. He once said to me, 'When everyone else is in top form, they improve my form.' He believed in teamwork."

—Richard Whorf
(director, *It Happened in Brooklyn*)

As Danny Webson Miller,
It Happened in Brooklyn, 1947.

"…Frank considers money of secondary importance. If memory serves me correctly, he gave at least a bulk of his salary for playing the priest In *Miracle of the Bells* to charity."

—Hedda Hopper (columnist)

ABOVE Half-sheet poster, *The Miracle of the Bells*, 1948.   **OPPOSITE** One-sheet poster, *The Kissing Bandit*, 1948.

"...ing *Ball Game* ... at MGM was pure joy and Frank was a ... lute delight to work with. He won my heart the first day or ... et when they had finished shooting a close-up of him over ... houlder. They were getting ready to move the camera for ... her shot when Frank said, "Wait a minute. What about my ... ?" And he made them reverse the camera angle and shoo ... -up over his shoulder, too.... [Gene] was concerned abou ... 's dancing ability so he made the steps as simple as he c ... they were dancing together. When we saw the movie, Fr ... than held his own. He danced up a storm."

... y Garrett (costar, *Take Me Out to the Ball Game*, 1949)

"On the Town is a motion picture done in the style of a smart Broadway review.....The numbers fairly zip along. The headliners form their own ensemble background as one by one each steps out for his particular specialty....Frank Sinatra's voice and harassed manner make his role a delight."

—*The Hollywood Reporter*
(review, *On the Town*, 1949)

LEFT Lobby cards, *On the Town*, 1949.
OPPOSITE With costars Jules Munshin and Gene Kelly.

"The first stumbling block was Frank Sinatra. Those were his famous days, and he was as hard to hide as the Statue of Liberty. He was always being mobbed. To get around that problem, we decided not to hire any limousines. Instead we hired yellow taxis. We would push Sinatra on the floor of the taxi…so that the taxi would seem empty. No, he didn't like that."

—Gene Kelly (costar, *On the Town*, 1949)

OPPOSITE With costar Gene Kelly, *On the Town*, 1949. ABOVE With costars Betty Garrett, Jules Munshin, Ann Miller, Gene Kelly, and Vera Ellen.

"Frank and I sang together…
and to balance our voices
he stood two feet from the
mike and I had to crawl in it.
What a voice that man has!"

—Jane Russell (costar, *Double Dynamite*, 1951)

ABOVE Lobby card, *Double Dynamite*, 1951.
RIGHT With costar Jane Russell.

Frank Sinatra as Johnny Dalton and Jane Russell as Mibs Goodhug:

JD: "And if we did get married, how would we manage? I have nothing. How would we live?"

MG: "I'm sure something would come along."

JD: "Yeah. And we'd have to feed that, too."

ABOVE With costar Groucho Marx in *Double Dynamite*. **OPPOSITE** With costar Jane Russell.

"I too had sat in the orchestra at the Paramount Theater when I was a teenager and screamed every time he opened his mouth. I was determined to keep my association with Mr. Sinatra as professional as possible. In retrospect, I suspect he wanted the same thing."

—Shelley Winters
(costar, *Meet Danny Wilson*, 1952)

OPPOSITE With costar Shelley Winters in *Meet Danny Wilson*, 1952.
RIGHT Lobby cards, *Meet Danny Wilson*.

"I loved it, it was a hell of a book. And then I spoke to Harry Cohn, who was then head of Columbia Pictures and a friend. He said, "Well, you've never done a dramatic role. You're the guy who sings and dances with Gene Kelly."

—Frank Sinatra

"He'd starred in half a dozen big pictures…and he'd lost it all. But he had the strength to start all over again completely from scratch. Being down in the business hadn't licked him as an individual. Maybe the whole world was saying he'd had it, but he didn't hear them or care."

—Sammy Davis, Jr.

OPPOSITE On set, *From Here to Eternity*.

"I knew I was the only actor to play Private Maggio, the funny and sour Italo-American. I knew Maggio. I went to high school with him in Hoboken. I was beaten up with him. I might have been Maggio."

—Frank Sinatra

RIGHT With costars Ernest Borgnine and Burt Lancaster, *From Here to Eternity*.

"As a singer…I rehearse and plan exactly where I'm going. But as an actor, I can't do that. To me, acting is reacting. If you set it up right, you can almost go without knowing every line….If I rehearse to death, I lose the spontaneity I think works for me….With Montgomery, though, I had to be patient because I knew that if I watched this guy, I'd learn something."

—Frank Sinatra

ABOVE With costar Montgomery Clift, *From Here to Eternity*. **OPPOSITE** On set, *From Here to Eternity*.

"Sinatra was at his best in the first or second take of a scene...whereas Clift would use each take as a rehearsal to add more detail so that the scenes gained in depth as we went on. It was an interesting problem when they did a scene together: how to get the best performance from them both in the same take."

—Fred Zinnemann (director, *From Here to Eternity*, 1953)

OPPOSITE On set, with costar Montgomery Clift, *From Here to Eternity*. **ABOVE** As Private Angelo Maggio, with Montgomery Clift. **OVERLEAF** On location in Honolulu, with Montgomery Clift and director Fred Zinnemann.

"His fervor, his anger, his bitterness had something to do with the character of Maggio, but also with what he had gone through in the last number of years: A sense of defeat, and the whole world crashing in on him.... You knew that this was a raging little man who was, at the same time, a good human being."

—Burt Lancaster (costar, *From Here to Eternity*, 1953)

ABOVE On set, with costars Montgomery Clift and Burt Lancaster, *From Here to Eternity*. **OPPOSITE** *From Here to Eternity*.

ABOVE On set with *From Here to Eternity* author James Jones and costar Montgomery Clift. OPPOSITE With costar Donna Reed.

"*From Here to Eternity* is being shown on a wide screen and with Stereophonic sound. It does not need these enhancements. It has scope, power and impact without them. It is the tale [among several entwined] of sinewy Angelo Maggio, enlisted man from the sidewalks of New York whose brave revolt against the confinements of the Army system ends in tragedy. Frank Sinatra is excellent in the non-singing role…a characterization rich in comic vitality and genuine pathos."

—A. H. Weiler
(*The New York Times*, review, *From Here to Eternity*, 1953)

OPPOSITE With costar Donna Reed, at the 26th Academy Awards, after accepting their Oscars for Best Supporting Actor and Best Supporting Actress for their performances in *From Here to Eternity*, March 25, 1954.

"He holds the screen and commands it with ease, authority and skill that is, obviously, the result of care, study, work, and an intelligent mind."

—*Cue* (review, *Suddenly*, 1954)

OPPOSITE With costar Nancy Gates, *Suddenly*, 1954. **RIGHT** Lobby cards, *Suddenly*.

"Frank was very conscious of his lack of [acting] training; he was never sure that he would be able to reproduce an effect more than once or twice because he had to rely on emotion more than craft."

—Robert Wagner

With director Lewis Allen on the set of *Suddenly*.

SUDDENLY – BY FRANK SINATRA, JR.

When *Suddenly* was released in 1954, *The New York Times* praised Frank Sinatra's performance as "a melodramatic tour de force." Indeed, *Suddenly* is an excellent picture, it is highly intense, and it contains one of the greatest performances Frank Sinatra ever gave in his dramatic career. At the time, Sinatra was still in his thirties and *Suddenly*, compared to some of the bigger pictures produced around then, was rather insignificant in the sense that it was low budget with a very small cast.

This was one of the biggest challenges Sinatra faced at that period in his life. Here was a man who had been in movies since 1942, when he was a band singer and one of the most popular crooners during the war years. Louis B. Mayer had picked him up and put him into MGM's regular staff of actors and musical performers, where he was teamed for several musicals with the great Gene Kelly. Those musicals were wonderful light entertainment, but in the process this young Frank Sinatra had the opportunity of working with and watching some excellent legitimate actors. One of the first was Lee J. Cobb.

Sinatra was very impressed with Cobb, and with the idea of acting dramatically in front of a movie camera. He always wanted to proceed further and it never really materialized until *From Here to Eternity* in 1953, when he won the Academy Award for the best performance of an actor in a supporting role. At the time, however, there were people who said that Sinatra's acting ability and his very good performance as Maggio were only a fluke, only an aberration, and could not be repeated.

Then, in 1954, came this low-budget script called *Suddenly*. Though it was originally offered to the great Montgomery Clift, Sinatra decided he was going to do it instead, to establish himself within the industry once and for all as a very good dramatic actor. Furthermore, because it was still in the days of the studio system, he chose this role so he could show the studio heads, producers, directors, and writers that he could be an actor capable of wearing different hats. Barely a year earlier, in *From Here to Eternity*, he had played a funny, innocuous, sympathetic character who died tragically and for whom you felt sorry. Now, he selected the role of John Baron, a man who was completely insane and, according to the script's notes, had not one redeeming quality. As a result, there was an overwhelming difference in Sinatra's style of acting—in the setup of his facial expressions, persona, body language, in the ghoulish pleasure on his face when he sets Sterling Hayden's broken arm. There was a protracted insanity. Everything about him was "Mr. Tough Guy."

Suddenly was a modestly budgeted picture. It begins with three FBI agents (including Frank Sinatra as John Baron) who arrive at the home of the Benson family in the town of Suddenly, California. They claim to be checking up on security prior to the arrival of the president of the United States on a train (or a streamliner as they were called when I was a boy) at a nearby station, but it quickly becomes clear that these men are not who they seem. It was filmed over four weeks in Newhall, California, now a densely populated area about fifty miles north of Los Angeles. There was virtually nothing there in 1954; it was to stand in for Small Town, Anywhere, USA. I know because I was there. I was only ten at the time, about a year older than Kim Charney, who played Pidge.

The film had a very accomplished cast and crew. The marvelous actor Sterling Hayden, who played Sheriff Tod Shaw, was tall and handsome and charismatic. He was described in those days as something of a "reluctant actor"—he was never really that comfortable on camera. Nancy Gates as Ellen Benson gave a magnificent performance. I can remember being on the sound stage and watching her. She retired early from films to raise a family. James Gleason was one of the unsung heroes of the movies. He played Pop Benson and later appeared with Robert Mitchum in the classic film *Night of the Hunter*. The malefactors, the bad guys, the guys in black were played by Christopher Dark and Paul Frees. Paul Frees became a very respected voice actor, perhaps best remembered for his work with Walt Disney and for portraying villain Boris Badenov on *The Rocky and Bullwinkle Show*. He became known as "The Man of a Thousand Voices." Willis Bouchey was very good and appeared in many, many films, usually as the doctor, the sheriff, the judge. The great celebrated composer David Raksin did the underscore in the soundtrack. He had previously done *The Bad and the Beautiful*, and his landmark *Laura* back in the '40s.

The wonderful Lewis Allen directed the film in a very simple fashion. From the beginning scene, from the opening optical credit, we are made aware that this is a specific type of movie. In the years that had passed, beginning in the late 1930s, the '40s, and even into the '50s, this particular look in a film became known as it is today in university history classes, and to people who study movies. It is "film noir"—characterized as being a dark kind of film. Richard Sale wrote the shooting script with a remarkable directness. There is no extraneous tissue; everything means something.

Almost the entire picture was shot in one room, which takes a lot of courage on the part of the producer, the writer, and the director. They have to have great faith in their cameramen and in their actors. The set creates a claustrophobia, a tautness in the tradition of the great suspense directors like John Ford and Alfred Hitchcock. The constant reference in the film to the faces of clocks gradually increases the tension. Compounding the situation is the fact that John Baron is agoraphobic: He hates crowds. Ellen Benson asks him, "Haven't you any feelings at all?" to which he answers, "No, I haven't, lady. They were taken out of me by experts. Feelings are a trap. Show me a guy with feelings and I'll show you a sucker. It's a weakness. Makes you think of something besides yourself. If I had any feelings left in me at all, it'd be for me. Just me. Before the war, I drifted and ran. Always lost in the great, big crowd. I used to dream about the crowd once in a while. I used to see all those faces scratching and shoving and biting. And then the mist would clear and somehow all those faces would be me. All me, and all nothing."

Early in the film a theme of anti-violence is established through the eyes of the mother, Ellen Benson, when she opposes Sheriff Shaw buying her son a cap pistol, because his father had died in the Korean war. She hates guns. She is totally nonviolent and raises her boy to be nonviolent. Her philosophy is pitted against John Baron's when, at one point, he makes her look down the barrel of the assassin's rifle. His philosophy is: "When you've got a gun, you are a sort of god. If you had the gun I'd be the chump and you'd be the god. The gun gives you the power of life and death. It's a funny sort of feeling to have control of life and death. . . . You could miss a man if you had a mind to. Or you could kill him dead in his tracks. And that made you a kind of god. And I liked it. Without the gun, I'm nothing. And I never had anything before I got one. First time I got one in my hands and killed a man, I got some self-respect. I was somebody." However, in the film's climax it is Ellen Benson who shoots him. The tough guy John Baron is revealed to have an Achilles' heel and at the end of his life he begs for mercy.

As an epilogue: Nine years after *Suddenly* was made, the unthinkable occurred when the then-president of the United States, John F. Kennedy, was murdered as he rode in his limousine in Dallas. That was November 22, 1963, and in the ensuing two weeks, a minor network official at ABC decided he was going to run *Suddenly* on network television while the people were still grieving from the horror of this tragedy. When word of this reached Sinatra he was absolutely incensed, one of the very few times that I had ever seen him that angry. He shot off a letter to the head of broadcasting at ABC, telling them that they should be jailed; that it was in such bad taste to do that just after the death of President Kennedy.

"As the assassin in the piece, Sinatra superbly refutes the idea that the straight-role potentialities which earned an Academy Award for him in *From Here to Eternity* was one-shot stuff. In *Suddenly*, the happy-go-lucky soldier of *Eternity* becomes one of the most repellent killers in American screen history. Sneeringly arrogant in the beginning, brokenly whimpering at the finish, Sinatra will astonish viewers who flatly resent bobby-soxers' idols."

—*Newsweek* (review, *Suddenly*, 1954)

PREVIOUS SPREAD With costars Sterling Hayden, James Gleason, Nancy Gates, and Kim Charney, *Suddenly*, 1954. OPPOSITE As John Baron, *Suddenly*.

c. 1954.

"…despite Frank's sure and rather cocky exterior, I always felt there was a sad vulnerability about him. I liked him. We had a fine relationship. There were many lovely things about him that I admired."

—Doris Day (costar, *Young at Heart*, 1954)

OPPOSITE One-sheet poster, *Young at Heart*, 1954. ABOVE With costar Doris Day.
OVERLEAF As Barney Sloan, *Young at Heart*.

[Doris, teary-eyed at the 75th birthday Frank arranged for Ethel Barrymore, called for a tissue and was hit in the forehead by a box of Kleenex tossed by a stagehand.] "Frank lunged for the guy, scolding, 'Don't ever do that! You don't throw things at a lady, understand?' Over the years whenever I pull a Kleenex out of a box, I think of Frank."

—Doris Day

ABOVE *Young at Heart*, 1954. OPPOSITE On set with costar Doris Day.

Young at Heart, 1954.

"One of his scenes . . . is a piece of satire on the medical profession, performed in front of his med school classmates between classes, while they await the arrival of their professor. He and I talked beforehand about the need for some comic relief at this point in a very serious story. He came up with the idea of a satire on a surgical operation. He did by it by going through elaborately exaggerated preparations, then performing a mock abdominal incision. This was a perfect expression of the very human, but still dangerous, sophomoric unseriousness about medicine that we wanted to show. Sinatra was an actor with far greater range than most people noticed. His fame as a singer and entertainer was so great that many assumed he could do nothing else. Not so."

—Stanley Kramer (director, *Not as a Stranger*, 1955)

ABOVE Half-sheet poster, *Not as a Stranger*, 1955. **OPPOSITE** With costar Olivia de Havilland.

"Never knocking himself out for a laugh, he plays the gambler as an earnest, worried man, with a peculiar idiom that comes naturally to him. He takes great pride in trivialities and his mind is forever seeking angles. He is always a man and never a buffoon. And. of course, the way he can tailor a Frank Loesser song is nobody's business but his own."

—Jack Moffit
(*The Hollywood Reporter*, review, *Guys and Dolls*, 1955)

"…the Detroit role is a breeze for Sinatra, and he plays it as casually as if he were eating a banana split."

—Louella Parsons (columnist)

With costars Johnny Silver and Stubby Kaye, *Guys and Dolls*.

ABOVE With costars Marlon Brando, Jean Simmons, and Vivian Blaine, *Guys and Dolls*. **OPPOSITE** With costar Marlon Brando. **OVERLEAF** With costars Marlon Brando, Jean Simmons, and Vivian Blaine. Photos by St. Hilaire.

"He got very quiet and seemed to be very, very far away and all of a sudden he sat back, and Brando, the great actor, said—you could barely hear him—'Boy, to be able to sing like that.'"

—Henry Silva (actor)

OPPOSITE With costar Sheldon Leonard, *Guys and Dolls*, 1955.
ABOVE With costars Marlon Brando, Jean Simmons, and Vivian Blaine.

115

RIGHT With costar Vivian Blaine, *Guys and Dolls*, 1955. OVERLEAF With Kim Novak, Lauren Bacall, and Humphrey Bogart, at the premiere of *The Desperate Hours*, Los Angeles, October 10, 1955.

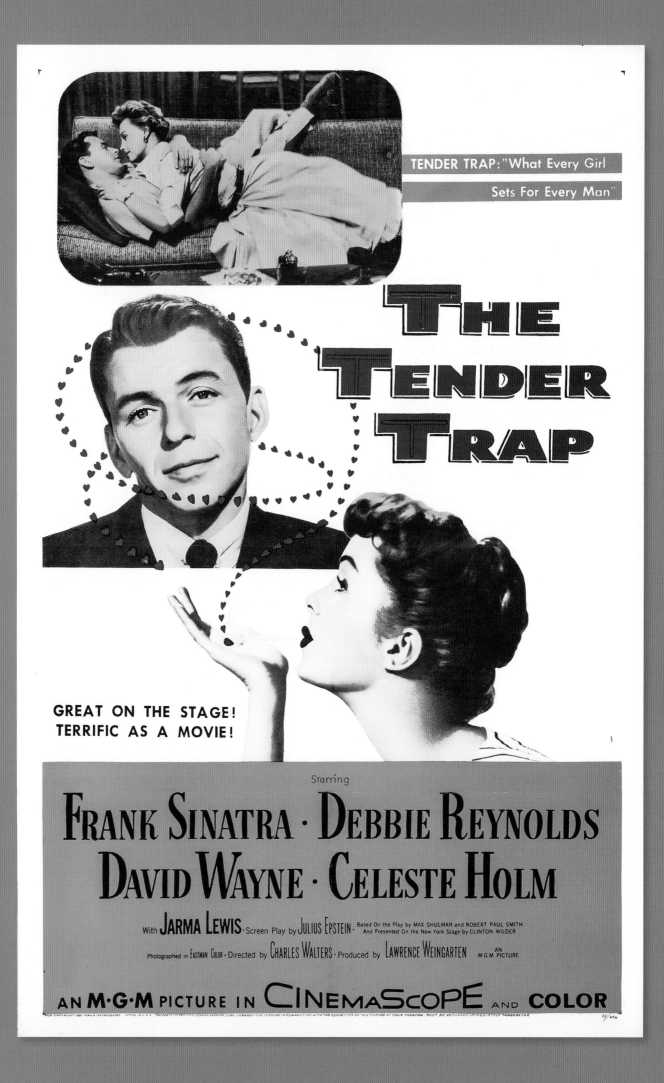

"*Tender Trap* is a cinch for top attendances everywhere; it's a great, GREAT comedy, magnificently written, wonderfully directed and acted. Colorful as a bright new lipstick and as merry as a sixth martini."

—*Hollywood Reporter*
(review, *The Tender Trap*, 1955)

OPPOSITE One-sheet poster, *The Tender Trap*, 1955.
RIGHT Lobby cards, *The Tender Trap*.

"…his performance is well-nigh a perfect demonstration of the sort of flippant, frantic thing he can do best. It catches the nervous, restless Frankie at the top of his comedy form."

—Bosley Crowther (*The New York Times*, review, *The Tender Trap*, 1955)

OPPOSITE With costar Debbie Reynolds, *The Tender Trap*.

BY NANCY SINATRA

It's impossible for me to choose one Frank Sinatra film, because my father gave so many fine performances, across every genre. Though there are several criteria one could employ to judge the merit of a movie, my personal measure is: "Will I watch it again?"

It is perhaps ironic, then, that some of my favorites among of my father's dramatic films are, at times, the most difficult for me to watch. One such film is *Von Ryan's Express*, a powerful story about the life in and the escape from a German prison camp. My father gives an action-packed performance as the resourceful air force colonel Joseph L. Ryan, determined to save the lives of his fellow POW soldiers even as it is clear his own life will be put in great danger. It's hard for me, when watching this film, to separate the man on screen from the man who is my father, and so there are moments in the film that seem all too real.

This seems appropriate to me; my father was always trying to find common ground with the characters he played, hoping to bring them vividly to life. In fact, one of the most striking examples of his immense devotion to the crafting of his characters actually took place during the filming of *Von Ryan's Express*: Dad actually convinced Richard Zanuck to alter the fate of his character, Colonel Ryan. He insisted, and Mr. Zanuck relented. Without giving anything away for those who have not seen the film, I truly believe that Dad was right.

Even beyond Dad's incredible performance, *Von Ryan's Express* is a beautiful film. The CinemaScope photography is gorgeous, the special effects and stunt work are ahead of their time, and under the skillful direction of Mark Robson, the action scenes had audiences of the day at the edge of their seats. Even though I might never be able to watch it again, this memorable film is burned on my brain. Mr. Robson knew exactly how to utilize two of my father's most lethal weapons on and off screen: his bright blue eyes and most expressive face.

In some cases, Dad first encountered the character he wanted to play in novels, even before he saw a script. I can remember seeing the books that would become some of his most recognized films in his library; those books included not only *Von Ryan's Express*, but also *From Here to Eternity* and Richard Condon's thriller *The Manchurian Candidate*. The actors in *The Manchurian Candidate* are brilliant, my father included. It's a riveting film from start to finish, but with an intelligence that resonates to this day. That being said, it's not a film that I watch again and again, because of its darker nature.

However, some of my father's musicals and comedies are films that I do watch very often. *A Hole in the Head*, for example, directed by Frank Capra. I even love the opening credits of this film, complete with a plane flying, glittering banners, and gorgeous aerial photography of a candy-colored Miami Beach.

In this film, my dad plays Tony, a down-on-his-luck small hotel owner about to lose everything. Only the love and devotion of his young son Ally (Eddie Hodges) holds him together and keeps him going. Too proud to accept help from anyone, Tony grasps at anything to try and dig himself out of the hole he has created, but to no avail. When he finally abandons all hope of a better life for himself and his son, Tony harshly pushes the boy toward what he believes will be a more stable life with Mario, Ally's uncle and Tony's brother, played by Edward G. Robinson. You can see the pain of failure and desperation in Dad's eyes; he didn't have to say a word. God, he was a good actor.

In typical Capra fashion, there is redemption for Tony in the end, and with the aid of glorious cinematography, the lovely Eleanor Parker, and a couple of terrific songs, it's a wonderful mix of laughter and tears that are the hallmarks of a Capra film. It's one of my favorites, and I can watch it again and again, though the honesty of my dad's performance breaks my heart.

Another favorite comedy of mine is *High Society*, a musical remake of the classic *The Philadelphia Story*. Dad is the second banana to Bing's lead, but it is more like a shared top spot. Their performance of "Well, Did You Evah?" has to be one of the most treasured screen duets of all time. It's also worth mentioning another great onscreen duet from the film, though it doesn't include Dad: "True Love" sung by Bing and the very beautiful Grace Kelly. The Cole Porter score is perfect for the cast. I could watch this movie every day and never tire of it.

Still, *The Tender Trap*, in which Dad costarred with Debbie Reynolds, is probably my true favorite of his movies. I thought Frank and Debbie were a perfect team, and wish they could have made more films together. There are scenes in this film where my father makes me laugh out loud. The fabulous production design by art directors Cedric Gibbons and Arthur Lonergan, along with set decorators Jack D. Moore and Edwin B. Willis, brings me back time and time again; they perfect the art of the mid-century bachelor pad, and use the color orange—well recognized as my dad's favorite hue. The costumes by Helen Rose are superb…no detail is ignored.

Of course I could not close this essay without mentioning a couple of the glorious early musicals Dad made, his wonderful vocals adding to their charm and ultimate success at the box office. The first movie I ever saw was *Anchors Aweigh*. I was about five years old, in Uncle Lew Wasserman's office at MCA with my friend, Lindy, Lew's daughter. We sat in the huge dark green leather chairs of the screening room, and it was thrilling to see my dad in Technicolor on the big screen. In those days Dad was the sidekick to Gene Kelly, and his dance pupil. In *Anchors Aweigh*, *On the Town*, and others, his rather shy characters did not get the leading lady, but the way Dad played the roles makes me wonder if it was those leading ladies who missed out.

Sheet music, *The Tender Trap*, 1955.

"A truly virtuoso performance. [Sinatra] has an incredible instinct for the look, the gesture, the shading of the voice that suggests tenderness, uncertainty, weakness, fatigue, despair."

—Arthur Knight (*Saturday Review*, review, *The Man With the Golden Arm*, 1955)

FRANK SINATRA · ELEANOR PARKER · KIM NOVAK

THE MAN WITH THE GOLDEN ARM

A FILM BY OTTO PREMINGER

With Arnold Stang, Darren McGavin, Robert Strauss, John Conte, Doro Merande, George E. Stone, George Mathews, Leonid Kinskey, Emile Meyer, Shorty Rogers, Shelly Manne, Screenplay by Walter Newman & Lewis Meltzer, From the novel by Nelson Algren, Music by Elmer Bernstein, Produced & Directed by Otto Preminger, Released by United Artists

ABOVE, OPPOSITE AND OVERLEAF As Frankie Machine, *The Man With the Golden Arm*, 1955.

"I was afraid that nobody out there could play it and that Preminger would crap it up. But Sinatra *was* Frankie Machine, just the way I wrote him in the book."

—Nelson Algren (author, *The Man With the Golden Arm*)

"My feeling toward Frank is one of admiration. He has seen so much that it is very interesting to be with him—and with his friends. They're bright, alert, and sharp—just as he is. The only way I could work with him on *Man With the Golden Arm*... was to know him only as the man he was playing. That way I could feel sorry for him and give him the sympathy which was needed. As soon as I walked on the set each day, I purposely forgot that we were friends."

—Kim Novak (costar, *The Man With the Golden Arm*)

OPPOSITE With costar Kim Novak, *The Man With the Golden Arm*. **ABOVE** With director Otto Preminger.

The Man With the Golden Arm.

"I would tease [Preminger] tremendously and he really loved it because nobody wanted to get involved with him because they were afraid he would chew you up. I had a lot of fun with Otto about his wonderful Vienna or Berlin accent. . . . I would ape him and he would say, 'Vy, vy you talk, I don't talk that vay, vy are you speaking that vay vith me.'"

—Frank Sinatra

ABOVE With director Otto Preminger, Sands casino owner and technical advisor Jack Entratter, and Robert Strauss, *The Man With the Golden Arm*. OPPOSITE Between takes, *The Man With the Golden Arm*.

"He was very compassionate about Kim's nervousness. He never complained and never made Kim feel that he was losing patience through any of it, even when we had to do key scenes over because of her anxiety."

—Otto Preminger
(director, *The Man With the Golden Arm*)

On set with director Otto Preminger, *The Man With the Golden Arm*.

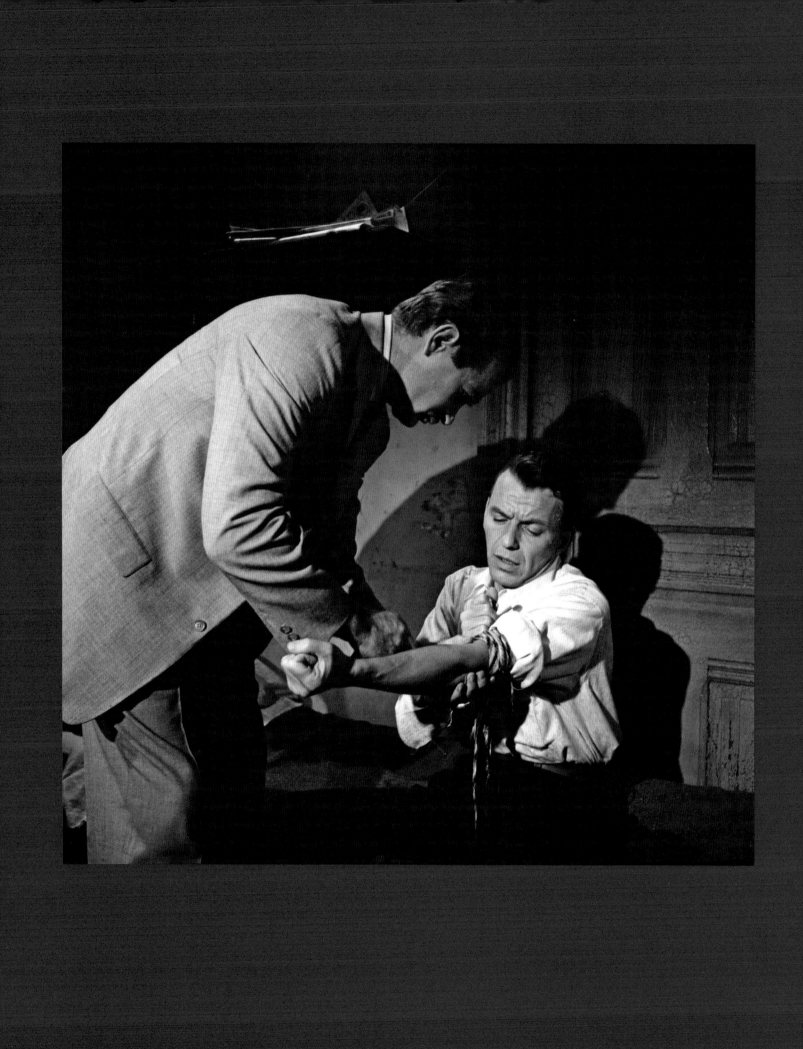

ABOVE With costar Darren McGavin **OPPOSITE** *The Man With the Golden Arm.*

"When I read the script, I thought this is a great piece of work and it's going to be tough to do. I got permission to watch a kid who was in the dryout position in a padded cell. The little guy must have weighed about ninety pounds, they were drying him out and he was trying to knock the walls down. I watched through a peephole, even though it was against the law. The poor kid was out of his head. I couldn't handle it, I walked away, I couldn't control myself. To see the actual thing was scary, but it helped me when we started shooting. I knew what I wanted to do."

—Frank Sinatra

OPPOSITE, ABOVE, AND OVERLEAF *The Man With the Golden Arm.*

To be sure, there are moments of amusement in this handsomely set and costumed film, which is served up in color and VistaVision....One stretch is where Frank Sinatra as the magazine writer sent to do a story on the mores of society plies the heroine with wine and somewhat unhooks her inhibitions. Mr. Sinatra makes hay with this scene."

—Bosley Crowther (*The New York Times*, review, *High Society*, 1956)

"There is one delightful duet…when Sinatra and Crosby get together for five minutes or so and show solid professionalism in their handling of 'What a Swell Party This Is.'"

—Bosley Crowther (*The New York Times*, review, *High Society*)

ABOVE With costars Bing Crosby and Grace Kelly, *High Society*. **OPPOSITE AND OVERLEAF** With costar Bing Crosby. Photo by Zinn Arthur.

"I'd always longed to do a musical and, of course, working with Bing and Frank was simply marvelous. They create a certain excitement and are two very strong personalities. So it was fascinating for me to be in the middle—watching the tennis match go back and forth from one to the other with tremendous wit and humor—each one trying to outdo the other...."

—Grace Kelly (costar, *High Society*)

OPPOSITE With costar Grace Kelly, *High Society*. **OVERLEAF** On set with costar Grace Kelly, *High Society*.

155

[On a visit to the set:] "Dad took me to lunch. Halfway through, a petite girl wearing blue jeans and a babushka came over to chat. She was in the movie, too. She was pale and pretty with a gentle voice—and Dad called her Gracie. He called her Gracie until the day she died even after Grace Kelly became 'Her Serene Highness, Princess Grace of Monaco,' to almost everyone else."

—Nancy Sinatra

ABOVE With costars Bing Crosby and Grace Kelly, *High Society*. OPPOSITE With director Charles Walters and costar Grace Kelly, *reviewing the song "You're Sensational" by Cole Porter, Los Angeles, January 17, 1956.*

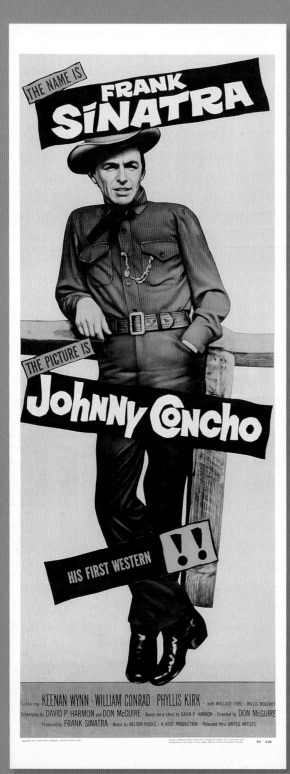

ABOVE Insert poster, *Johnny Concho*, 1956. **RIGHT** *As Johnny Concho*. Photograph taken as reference for poster art.

"In 1956 [Hollywood publicist Warren] Cowan was determined to shine a light on Sinatra's first western, *Johnny Concho*. He came up with the idea of recruiting a western star to serve as the film's technical adviser. Sinatra hardly knew Gary Cooper, and Cowan himself had never met him. But that didn't stop Cowan from calling up Cooper, introducing himself, and making the pitch. A week later, with 36 members of the press on hand, Cooper walked onto the set and shook Sinatra's hand. News organizations here and abroad wrote about it for weeks."

—*Los Angeles Magazine*

OPPOSITE With costar Phyllis Kirk, *Johnny Concho*. **ABOVE** With Gary Cooper, on set, *Johnny Concho*.

"…Sinatra arrived and Kramer brought him over. Standing there with Cary Grant on one side of me and Frank Sinatra on the other, I said to myself, It's not possible that this is happening. How do you do, Frank Sinatra, but it is not happening to me but somebody else and I am having this dream and watching it happen. Before I came to Spain, I hear all sorts of things. He is moody, he is difficult, he is a tiger, he fights. Here he is kindly, friendly. He has even helped me with my English, has teached me how people really speak in Hollywood. He is a regular gasser. I dig him."

—Sophia Loren (costar, *The Pride and the Passion*, 1957)

OPPOSITE One-sheet, *The Pride and the Passion*, 1957. **OVERLEAF** On location in Spain with director Stanley Kramer and costar Sophia Loren, *The Pride and the Passion*.

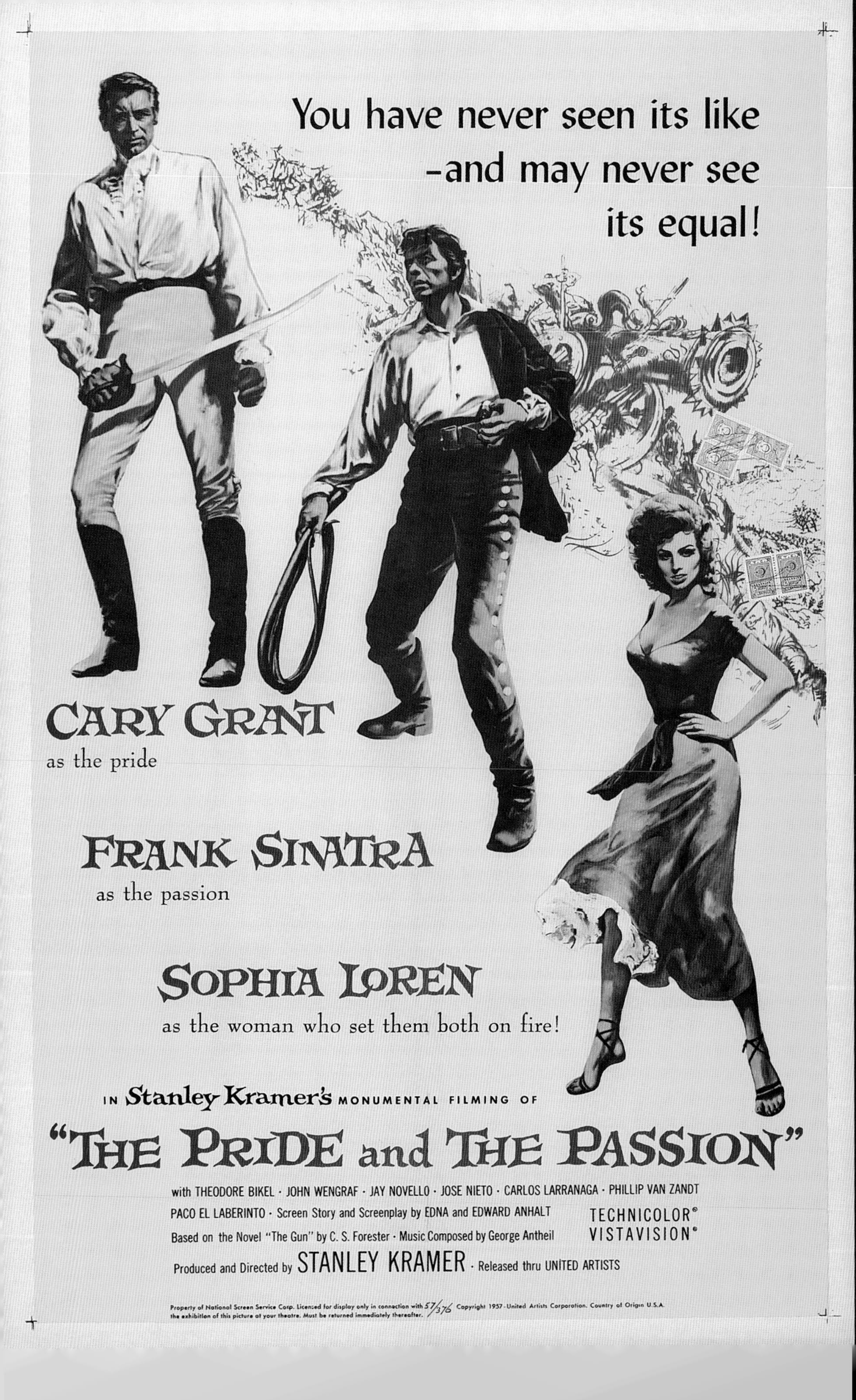
You have never seen its like
–and may never see
its equal!
CARY GRANT
as the pride
FRANK SINATRA
as the passion
SOPHIA LOREN
as the woman who set them both on fire!
IN Stanley Kramer's MONUMENTAL FILMING OF
"THE PRIDE and THE PASSION"
with THEODORE BIKEL · JOHN WENGRAF · JAY NOVELLO · JOSE NIETO · CARLOS LARRANAGA · PHILLIP VAN ZANDT
PACO EL LABERINTO · Screen Story and Screenplay by EDNA and EDWARD ANHALT
Based on the Novel "The Gun" by C. S. Forester · Music Composed by George Antheil
TECHNICOLOR®
VISTAVISION®
Produced and Directed by STANLEY KRAMER · Released thru UNITED ARTISTS
Property of National Screen Service Corp. Licensed for display only in connection with the exhibition of this picture at your theatre. Must be returned immediately thereafter.
57/376
Copyright 1957-United Artists Corporation. Country of Origin U.S.A.

PARAMOUNT presents
FRANK SINATRA
MITZI GAYNOR JEANNE CRAIN
EDDIE ALBERT
The Joker is Wild
A CHARLES VIDOR PRODUCTION
BEVERLY GARLAND · JACKIE COOGAN
DIRECTED BY CHARLES VIDOR
PRODUCED BY SAMUEL J. BRISKIN
SCREENPLAY BY OSCAR SAUL
FROM A BOOK BY ART COHN
BASED ON THE LIFE OF JOE E. LEWIS
VISTAVISION
A PARAMOUNT RELEASE
Copyright 1957 Paramount Pictures Corporation. Country of Origin U.S.A.
—10715—
57 \428

"The objective was a true representation of pixie Lewis, bon-vivant and nitery buffoon and acknowledged by many in the trade as doyen of the saloon comedians. It doesn't matter much about this objective, for the fact is that the finished product is a pretty good picture.... Sinatra obviously couldn't be made to look like Lewis; any thought of a reasonable facsimile, appearance-wise, is out of the question. And Lewis's style of delivery is unique and defies accurate copying [although some of his onstage mannerisms are aped by the film's star quite well]. But these are minor reservations in light of the major job Sinatra does at being an actor. He's believable and forceful—alternately sympathetic and pathetic, funny and sad."

—*Variety* (review, *The Joker Is Wild*, 1957)

OPPOSITE As Joe E. Lewis, *The Joker Is Wild*.

"Sinatra and I, my god, we got on wonderfully. We had great times together. When he came in, he had complete concentration. When he's in that scene, you could shoot a gun off, he wouldn't hear it."

—George Sidney
(director, *Pal Joey*, 1957)

LEFT *Pal Joey*, 1957. OPPOSITE As Joey Evans,
Pal Joey. Photo by Zinn Arthur.

"The show is saved by Frank Sinatra, who does a tremendous job in the title role. Sinatra does not dance a step in the film, but somehow he crowds the screen with rhythm every time he moves."

— *Time* (review, *Pal Joey*)

"You treat a lady like a dame, and a dame like a lady."

—Frank Sinatra (as "Joey Evans" in *Pal Joey*)

ABOVE Soundtrack album cover, *Pal Joey*, 1957. **OPPOSITE** Photo by Sid Avery. **OVERLEAF** *Pal Joey*.

AS BIG AND BRAVE AND BOLD A LOVE STORY AS HAS EVER BEEN EXPLODED ON THE SCREEN!

The FRANK ROSS Production

FRANK **SINATRA!** TONY **CURTIS!** NATALIE **WOOD!**

in

Kings Go Forth

with LEORA DANA

From the novel "Kings Go Forth" by JOE DAVID BROWN · Directed by DELMER DAVES
Screenplay by MERLE MILLER · Music by ELMER BERNSTEIN
Released thru UNITED UA ARTISTS

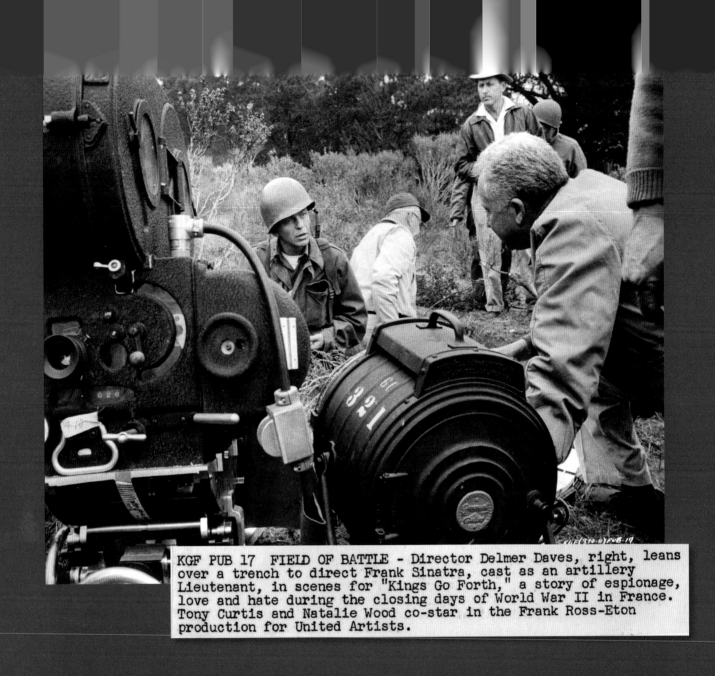

KGF PUB 17 FIELD OF BATTLE - Director Delmer Daves, right, leans over a trench to direct Frank Sinatra, cast as an artillery Lieutenant, in scenes for "Kings Go Forth," a story of espionage, love and hate during the closing days of World War II in France. Tony Curtis and Natalie Wood co-star in the Frank Ross-Eton production for United Artists.

"The Thin Singer has never had a more difficult role and he has never more completely mastered a characterization. Might as well admit it, he's a great actor. He makes you love and understand the Yankee lieutenant, a cynical man hardly able to believe himself that he has fallen tenderly in love with a young half-negress, puzzled by the friendship he feels for the GI 'pal' he intuitively recognizes as a heel."

—Dorothy Manners
(*Los Angeles Examiner*, review, *Kings Go Forth*, 1958)

KGF PUB 19 MEET THE CHAMPS - Frank Sinatra and Tony Curtis, teamed in the United Artists film "Kings Go Forth," exhibit proudly the gold cups presented them as respectively best martini mixer and best amateur barber in the film industry. Cups were presented by their respective stand-ins -- who obviously know on which side their bread is buttered!

KGF PUB 18 LAST MINUTE BRUSH-UP -- Locationing near Carmel, California, while filming "Kings Go Forth" for United Artists Frank Sinatra and Natalie Wood take a last glance at the script before facing Director Delmer Daves cameras. Tony Curtis co-stars in the Frank Ross-Eton production.

KGF PUB 16 STUDY TIME - Frank Sinatra concentrates on lines for an upcoming scene on the set of United Artists "Kings Go Forth" in which he is teamed with Tony Curtis and Natalie Wood with Delmer Daves directing the Fr ank Ross-Eton production.

KGF PUB 15 CELEBRITY SALUTE -- Visiting Frank Sinatra during filming of "Kings Go Forth" for United Artists in Hollywood, Cabaret Star Sammy Davis Jr. hops to attention at sight of the seven-star general's hat worn as a gag by Sinatra (who plays a lieutenant in the Frank Ross-Eton production). Tony Curtis and Natalie Wood co-star in the film directed by Delmer Daves.

OPPOSITE Costar Natalie Wood and Robert Wagner give Frank Sinatra a close-up look at Natalie's engagement ring, December 10, 1957. **CLOCKWISE FROM TOP LEFT** With costar Tony Curtis, with costar Natalie Wood, with Sammy Davis, Jr., and on set, *King's Go Forth*.

"A friend to me has no race, no class, and belongs to no minority. My friendships were formed out of affection, mutual respect, and a feeling of having something strong in common. These are eternal values that cannot be racially classified. This is the way I look at race. I'd personally like to see more friendships forged across color and religious lines, for I feel this is the surest way to erase all the lines that divide people everywhere."

—Frank Sinatra (to *Ebony* magazine)

OPPOSITE With costar Natalie Wood and a stand-in for costar Tony Curtis. Photographs taken as reference for poster art, *King's Go Forth*, 1958.

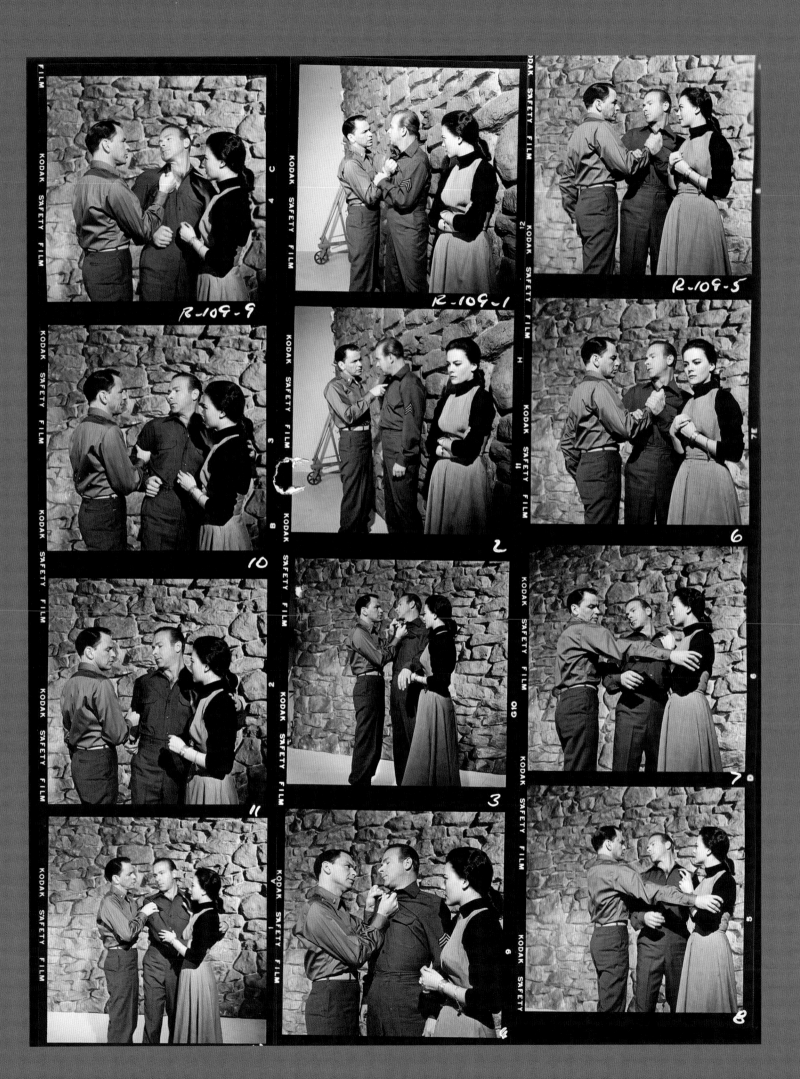

From the bold, new novel by the author of "From Here To Eternity"

FRANK SINATRA

DEAN MARTIN

SHIRLEY MacLAINE

M-G-M presents
A SOL C. SIEGEL PRODUCTION

..."SOME CAME RUNNING"

With

MARTHA HYER

ARTHUR KENNEDY

NANCY GATES

LEORA DANA • Screen Play by JOHN PATRICK and ARTHUR SHEEKMAN
Based on the Novel by JAMES JONES • In CinemaScope and METROCOLOR • Directed by VINCENTE MINNELLI

Frank had swagger and a command that intimidated people and rightfully earned him the title 'Chairman of the Board.' He could also, however, be extremely vulnerable and exceedingly generous in his appreciation of someone else's talent. I always thought he was responsible for my good performance in *Some Came Running*. 'Let the kid be killed,' he said to Vincente Minnelli [the director] and to the head of the studio. 'If she dies, she'll get more sympathy. Then she'll get nominated.' He was right."

—Shirley MacLaine (costar, *Some Came Running*, 1958)

OPPOSITE One-sheet poster, *Some Came Running*, 1958. OVERLEAF With costar Shirley MacLaine.

"A thoroughly fresh, aggressive and sardonic comedy…The prize goes to Sinatra who makes the hero of this film a soft-hearted, hard-boiled, white-souled black sheep whom we will cherish, along with Mr. Deeds and Mr. Smith, as one of the great guys that Mr. Capra has escorted to the American screen."

—Bosley Crowther
(*The New York Times*, review, *A Hole in the Head*, 1959)

A Hole in the Head, 1959.

"Sinatra manages to arouse sympathy without employing sentimentality; [Edward G.] Robinson displays such finesse as a broad comedy foil that he almost steals the show from Sinatra. Not quite, of course. No one these days ever completely steals the show from Sinatra."

—*Newsweek*
(review, *A Hole in the Head*)

With Kipp Hamilton, at a promotional event for *A Hole in the Head*, May 1959.

"He kept saying, 'Give the close-up to Steve.' He went out of his way to give me the breaks. 'It's your picture, kid.'"

—Steve McQueen (costar, *Never So Few*, 1959)

ABOVE With costar Gina Lollobrigida, *Never So Few*, 1959. **OPPOSITE** One-sheet poster, *Never So Few*.

ビルマルート制覇をめぐる激烈な戦場に咲いた非情の恋！

総天然色
シネマスコープ

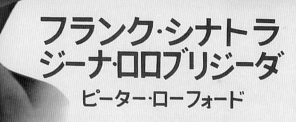

NEVER SO FEW

フランク・シナトラ
ジーナ・ロロブリジーダ
ピーター・ローフォード

戦雲

監督 ジョン・スタージェス

M·G·M超特作

Can Can

di COLE PORTER

FRANK SINATRA · SHIRLEY Mac LAINE
MAURICE CHEVALIER e LOUIS JOURDAN

NELLA PRODUZIONE DI JACK CUMMINGS

CON JULIET PROWSE   REGIA DI WALTER LANG   PRODUTTORE ASSOCIATO SAUL CHAPLIN

SCENEGGIATURA DI DOROTHY KINGSLEY e CHARLES LEDERER

PRODOTTO DALLA "SUFFOLK-CUMMINGS PRODUCTIONS,,

DISTRIBUZIONE

20th CENTURY FOX

CINEMASCOPE   TECHNICOLOR

DEAR FILM

Vecchioni & Guadagno - Via del Casale de Merode, 8 - Roma - Aprile 1965

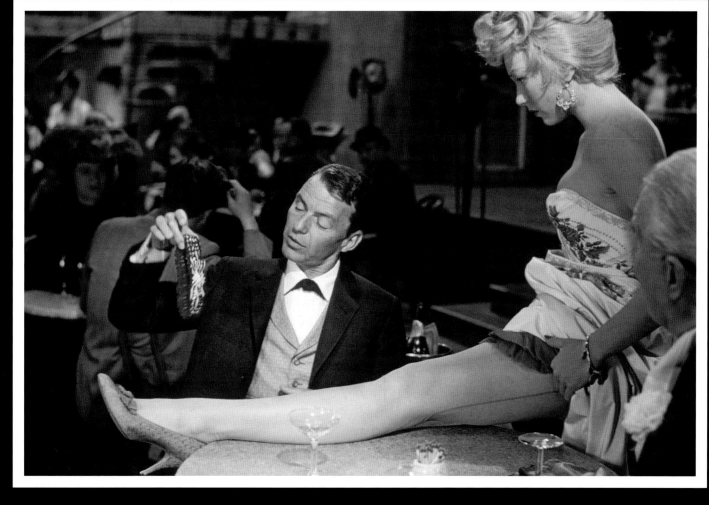

"Perhaps because his role was written specifically for him, Sinatra is Sinatra, ring-a-ding-ding and all. His naturalness makes him all the more effective, and his charm and self-assuredness ably complement a vocal style which fits hand in glove with the Porter tunes, particularly 'It's All Right with Me.'"

—*Variety* (review, *Can-Can*, 1960)

"Being condemned by Khrushchev may be an even bigger commercial asset than being banned in Boston, for *Can-Can*, whose dancing the Russian premier pronounced 'immoral' when he saw it on the Hollywood set last fall, opened last week with an advance sale reportedly bigger than the supercolossal *Ben-Hur*'s. The show itself, in color and Todd-AO, turns out to be lavish, easy to look at, and … Chevalier and Sinatra are entertaining with their individual, off-hand brands of charm…."

—*Newsweek* (1960)

OPPOSITE With costar Shirley MacLaine, *Can-Can*. OVERLEAF (from left to right) With costars Richard Conte, Buddy Lester, Joey Bishop, Sammy Davis, Jr., Dean Martin, Peter Lawford, Akim Tamiroff, Richard Benedict, Henry Silva, Norman Fell, and Clem Harvey, *Ocean's 11*, 1960.

cognizing the potential in our
mbination, he formulated 'The Five-
ar Plan': Assuming things continued
it seemed they would, we'd make
e pictures together, one a year."

Sammy Davis, Jr. (costar, *Ocean's 11*)

ABOVE *Ocean's 11*. **RIGHT** With costars Sammy Davis, Jr., Dean Martin, and Joey Bishop on the set of *Ocean's 11*, 1960. Photo by Sid Avery.

"Frank called me one day and said that he and his pack were doing a picture in Las Vegas and they wanted me to play a bit part of an inebriated New Year's Eve celebrant. . . . No money . . . no billing . . . but they would give me a

ABOVE With costars Dean Martin, Peter Lawford and Sammy Davis, Jr., *Ocean's 11*.

new car for less than five minutes' work....
I took a brief break, long enough to fly to Vegas
to do the cameo, not for the car, but to be with
old friends, Frank, Dean, and Sammy."

—Shirley MacLaine (costar, *Ocean's 11*)

"This is such an enormous talent. Frank had some kind of magic that a lot of us wish we had."

—Peter Lawford (costar, *Ocean's 11*, 1960)

On set with costar Peter Lawford and director Lewis Milestone, *Ocean's 11*. Photo by Floyd McCarty.

"Frank was notorious for not wanting to do a scene again. I've never known a man who knew exactly what was right for him at all times. And so when he felt he had a scene right, he didn't have to question it. We got to the end of this scene, and he gets up to go and he went out. Kept right on going—didn't wait for 'Okay, that's good' or 'Let's try it again.' And I said, 'Frank! Maybe I wasn't very good. We need another one.' He was beyond earshot. He was gone."

—Angie Dickinson (costar, *Ocean's 11*, 1960)

OPPOSITE With costars Dean Martin and Peter Lawford, *Ocean's 11*.
OVERLEAF On set, with director Lewis Milestone, *Ocean's 11*.

"…a very special gang of Hollywood rebels, the innest in-group in the world. 'The Clan,' as they've been dubbed by others, possess talent, charm, romance, and a devil-may-care nonconformity that gives them immense popular appeal—so much so that today they sit at the very top of the Hollywood star system, with Sinatra the king of the hill.…"

—*Playboy* (review, *Ocean's 11*)

ABOVE *Ocean's 11* world premiere event, Las Vegas, 1960. **OPPOSITE** With costars Dean Martin and Peter Lawford at the *Ocean's 11* world premiere event.

In the great high-adventure tradition of "The Guns Of Navarone" and "The Bridge On The River Kwai"!

SPENCER TRACY AND **FRANK SINATRA**

in the MERVYN LeROY · FRED KOHLMAR production

THE DEVIL AT 4 O'CLOCK

KERWIN MATHEWS · JEAN-PIERRE AUMONT · GREGOIRE ASLAN · ALEXANDER SCOURBY · BARBARA LUNA · LIAM O'BRIEN · BASED ON THE NOVEL BY MAX CATTO · **MERVYN LeROY** · **FRED KOHLMAR** · EASTMAN COLOR · COLUMBIA PICTURES RELEASE

problem was that Sinatra would only work in the [afte]rnoon. In the morning he hired a private plane and [hop]ped from island to island trying to convince the star [inh]abitants to vote for Kennedy in the next presidential [ele]ction. Around two o'clock he returned, exhausted, a[t the] precise moment when Tracy was retiring for the day [in h]is room. How, in these conditions, the scenes betwe[en Tra]cy and Sinatra were shot is a mystery to me."

[Je]an-Pierre Aumont (costar, *The Devil at 4 O'Clock*, 1961)

[O]n location in Maui, Hawaii, with costar Spencer Tracy, *The Devil [at 4 O'C]lock*, 1961. **ABOVE** Half-sheet poster, *The Devil at 4 O'Clock*

FRANK SINATRA · DEAN MARTIN
PETER LAWFORD · SAMMY DAVIS

3 SARGENTOS

DIRIGIDA POR JOHN STURGES

PANAVISION · TECHNICOLOR

"The next film The Clan did together was *Sergeants 3*. We all trooped over to a place in Utah and met up with the producer, Howard Koch. [Frank] made seven films for Koch and they remained good friends. Howard always understood that Frank needs excitement. He doesn't like hanging around, waiting for things to happen. But he also knew that Frank was highly conscientious. *Ocean's 11* was a lot of fun, but I think *Sergeants 3* was the best film we ever did together. [It was Frank] who showed me there is a special way to ride a horse in a western. To make it good for the camera, you have to sit high and straight on the saddle. He knew that slouching on the screen looks dreadful. You tighten up the stirrups so you don't bounce up and down. You also try to hold the saddle horn, especially if you are riding away from the camera. Getting on and off a horse is more important than anything else. It can be extremely undignified unless you have the knack. Some people could never master it."

—Sammy Davis, Jr. (costar, *Sergeants 3*, 1962)

OPPOSITE On location in Kanab, Utah, *Sergeants 3*. OVERLEAF Sinatra having his portrait painted on set.

"*Sergeants 3* was one of the happiest experiences of my life, because I was the baby doll on the set with all of those guys. I had a wonderful time but, unfortunately, they all treated me like their kid sister. Dean was great to be around. They all sipped pretty good, but I never saw him sloshed. In fact, he taught me to drink beer on the rocks. And Frank taught me to drink champagne the same way."

—Ruta Lee (costar, *Sergeants 3*)

ABOVE On set, *Sergeants 3*. OPPOSITE With costar Dean Martin between takes on location in Kanab, Utah. OVERLEAF With costar Dean Martin (during a break while filming *Sergeants 3*) visiting Audrey Hepburn, director William Wyler, and Shirley MacLaine on the set of *The Children's Hour*, 1961.

If you come in five minutes after this picture begins, you won't know what it's all about!

when you've seen it all, you'll swear there's never been anything like it!

Frank Sinatra
Laurence Harvey
Janet Leigh

The Manchurian Candidate

co-starring

Angela Lansbury Henry Silva James Gregory

Produced by GEORGE AXELROD and JOHN FRANKENHEIMER Directed by JOHN FRANKENHEIMER

Screenplay by GEORGE AXELROD Based upon a Novel by RICHARD CONDON Executive Producer HOWARD W. KOCH

An M. C. PRODUCTION RELEASED THRU UNITED ARTISTS

There was some opposition from United Artists because [studio president] Arthur Krim wanted to be ambassador to Israel, and he didn't think President Kennedy would want it made. It turned out that Sinatra was very friendly with him. President Kennedy asked what he was going to do next, and Sinatra said, 'I want to do *Manchurian Candidate.'* And the president said, 'God I love that book. Who's gonna play the mother?'"

—John Frankenheimer (director, *The Manchurian Candidate*, 1962)

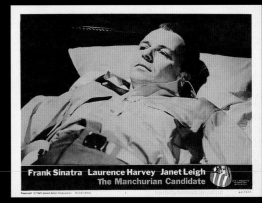

OPPOSITE Insert poster, *The Manchurian Candidate*, 1962.
RIGHT Lobby cards, *The Manchurian Candidate*.

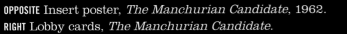

PLEASE CREDIT
"THE MANCHURIAN CANDIDATE"
A M.C. Production for
United Artists release

LEFT As Major Bennett Marco, *The Manchurian Candidate.* **ABOVE** With costars
Janet Leigh and Laurence Harvey, *The Manchurian Candidate.*

From: Mort Nathanson
        United Artists Corp.
        729 Seventh Ave., N.Y.C.
        CIrcle 5-6000

"THE MANCHURIAN CANDIDATE"
PRELIMINARY FACT SHEET

"The Manchurian Candidate" stars Frank Sinatra, Laurence Harvey, Janet Leigh, Angela Lansbury, Henry Silva and James Gregory.

The word which keynotes this production is unusual. It is designed to carry the utmost in suspense and thrills against an unusual dramatic story. Stars and glamour fade into the background as the picture unfolds a fantastic tale which builds in suspense until the moviegoer's hair is standing on end. The drama is profound, the love scenes exciting and the action high powered.

Essentially, it is a tale of horror, a nightmare, but yet it flickers with truths and hair-raising doubts. As a drama, it is filled with soul-searching, love, murder, greed and humor. It ranges from a battlefield in Korea to a major political party's national convention in Madison Square Garden.

The picture, an M.C. Production, is a joint venture between producers George Axelrod's and John Frankenheimer's companies and Frank Sinatra's Essex Productions. United Artists will release the picture in November (around election time).

(more)

From: Mike Hutner
       United Artists Corp.
       729 Seventh Ave., N.Y.C.
       CIrcle 5-6000

"THE MANCHURIAN CANDIDATE"

(Production Story)

Shortly after Richard Condon's second novel, "The Manchurian Candidate," was published, many of Hollywood's top actors sought it as a vehicle to star themselves. Robert Mitchum was so enthused that he discussed the idea of making it into a film with Frank Sinatra. The big drawback was how to adapt it for the screen. Sinatra, among others, was greatly impressed, but he, also, couldn't see how a writer could tackle it with the script problems entailed in translating it to the screen. Hollywood let the novel rest until a young team of daring creative geniuses took hold of the property and fashioned it into an exciting project.

George Axelrod, famed for his movie ("Breakfast at Tiffany's," "Seven Year Itch," etc.) hits, and stage ("Will Success Spoil Rock Hunter?" and "Seven Year Itch") hits, got together with five-time TV Emmy Award nominee and film director ("All Fall Down," "Bird Man of Alcatraz" and "The Young Savages") John Frankenheimer.

Axelrod and Frankenheimer again took the property, after years of preparing it, to Frank Sinatra. Right after he read the script, he agreed that it more than effectively brought to the screen the same suspense and drama with which Condon's writing so successfully engrossed the reading public. The picture, an M.C.

(more)

The Manchurian Candidate.

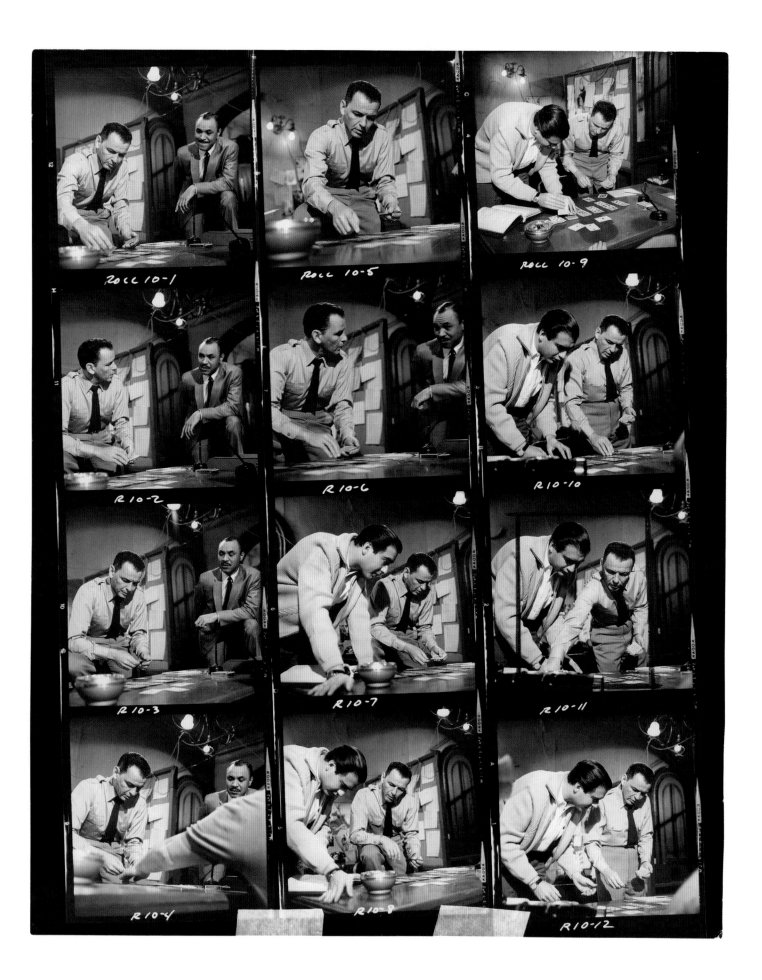

Roll 10-1
Roll 10-5
Roll 10-9
R 10-2
R 10-6
R 10-10
R 10-3
R 10-7
R 10-11
R 10-4
R 10-8
R 10-12

ABOVE AND OPPOSITE With director John Frankenheimer, *The Manchurian Candidate*.

"I was amazed how conscientious Frank is and how hard he worked. We had rehearsals before we started shooting and Frank always had suggestions. I think he's an actor who needs a challenge."

—Janet Leigh (costar, *The Manchurian Candidate*)

OPPOSITE On set with costar Janet Leigh, *The Manchurian Candidate*. **ABOVE** With costar Janet Leigh, promotional photo with original grease pencil markings for later retouching, *The Manchurian Candidate*. **OVERLEAF** On set with producer Howard W. Koch, unidentified man, costar Laurence Harvey, and screenwriter George Axelrod.

"He was very serious about his work; he went over his wardrobe, the look of the film, the dramatic arc. He didn't just pick up a script.... He prepared; I saw him in thrall to the words of *The Manchurian Candidate*."

—Robert Wagner

OPPOSITE On location, *The Manchurian Candidate*. **ABOVE** On location, with photographer William Read Woodfield.

"…the film is artfully contrived, the plot so interestingly started, the dialogue so racy and sharp, and John Frankenheimer's direction so exciting in the style of Orson Welles when he was making *Citizen Kane*…that the fascination of it is strong."

—Bosley Crowther (*The New York Times*, review, *The Manchurian Candidate*)

"Frank Sinatra is an extremely effective performer who has played the character that he has devised for himself. That works wonderfully well for him, and sometimes he takes a good step beyond that. He did in *The Manchurian Candidate*. He's very good in it. I think it was one of best performances I ever saw him give."

—Angela Lansbury
(costar, *The Manchurian Candidate*)

The Manchurian Candidate.

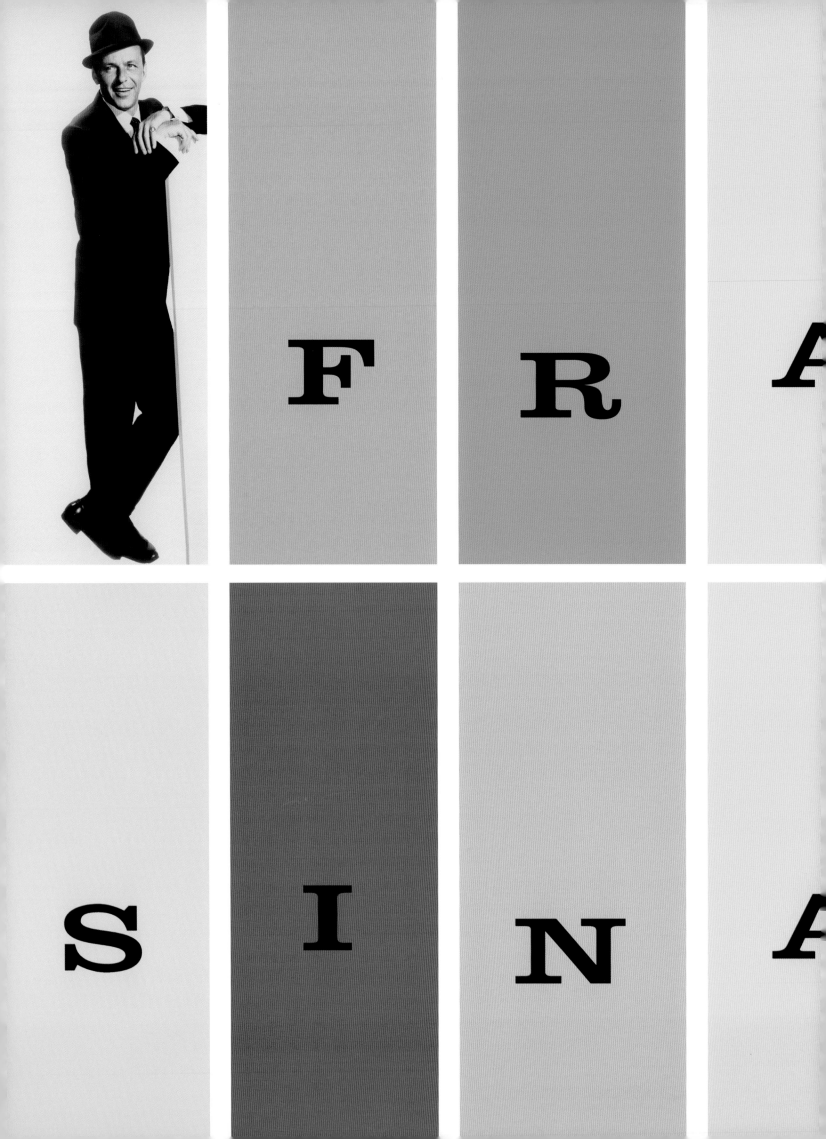

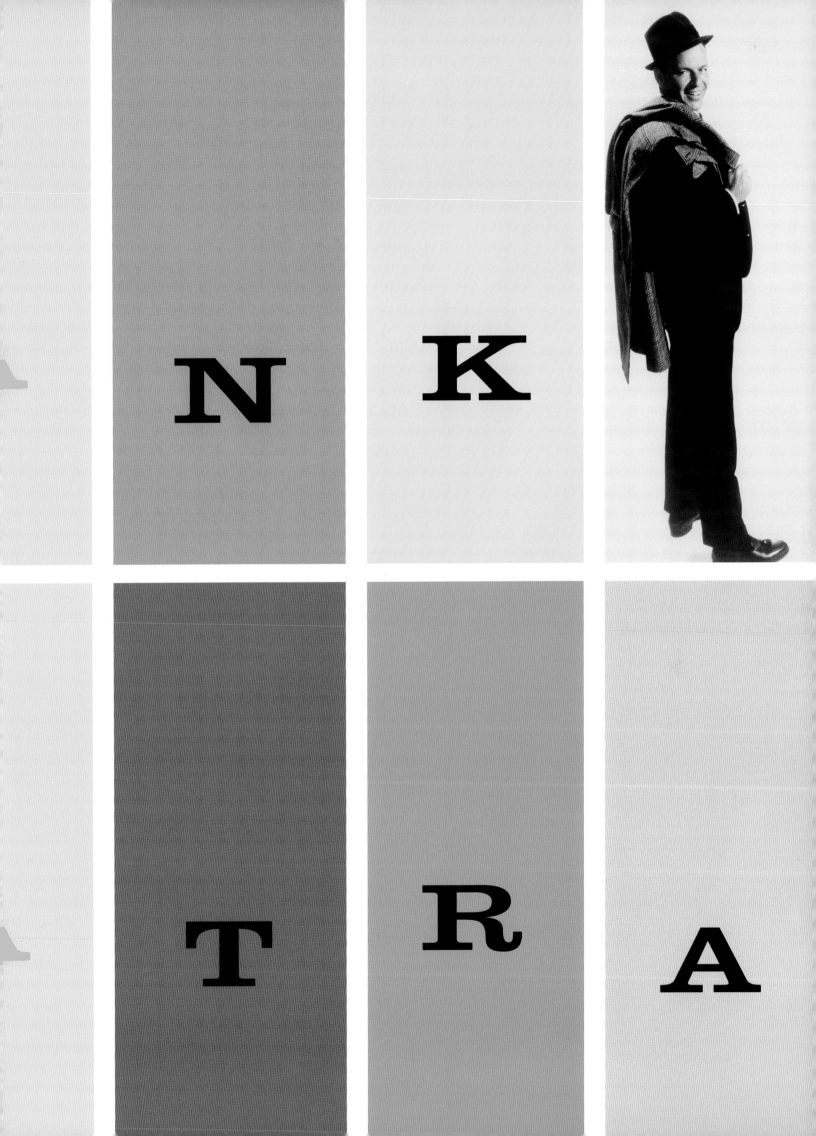

FRANK SINATRA in '**COME BLOW YOUR HORN**' (A) A Paramount Release Executive Producer HOWARD W. KOCH
Co-starring **LEE J. COBB · MOLLY PICON · BARBARA RUSH · JILL ST. JOHN** and introducing **TONY BILL** ·Technicolor'·Panavision'

"Frank was terrific. I enjoyed working with him....He had a certain impatience, a certain desire to get moving....In those days, films and lenses weren't as fast as they are today. You really had to wait for the light to be bright. He had the music piped into his ear, so he could be mouthing the tune he was listening to. My assistant was on a walkie-talkie....I kept hearing, 'How soon are we going to go?' I knew these questions were coming from Frank....We cued the music. He came out of the door onto the street. People were walking by and didn't realize it was Frank Sinatra, singing. He walked the block, stepped off the curb, flagged the first taxi that came along—and was gone for the day."

—Bud Yorkin (director, *Come Blow Your Horn*, 1963)

OPPOSITE With director Bud Yorkin and composer Nelson Riddle (at piano), *Come Blow Your Horn*, 1963.
ABOVE Lobby card, with (left to right) costars Barbara Rush, Phyllis McGuire, and Jill St. John. *Come Blow Your Horn*. OVERLEAF With costars Anita Ekberg, Dean Martin, and Ursula Andress, *4 for Texas*, 1963.

"We were in the cemetery, burying Edward G. Robinson, who played my father. Howard Koch drove into the cemetery and said, 'I want you to know President Kennedy has been shot.' Sinatra shut down the shoot for the day and briefly considered closing down the entire production."

—Barbara Rush (costar, *Robin and the 7 Hoods*, 1964)

OPPOSITE *Robin and the 7 Hoods*, 1964. **ABOVE** One-sheet poster, *Robin and the 7 Hoods*.

"Working on that picture was a blast. Off-camera, the boys, as Frank called them, were just like you see them onstage—loose and easy—plenty of laughs and one big surprise. I didn't notice when I first read the script. As I mentioned, the movie was a musical and Sammy Cahn, the best composer in the business . . . tapped me on the shoulder. I was bent over inspecting the doughnuts. He told me he wrote a song for me to sing. I was aghast—terrified—I can't sing— can't carry a tune. 'Oh no, no, Sam, no song—no singing, not me.' Later that day, Sinatra summed it up: 'You're worried you can't sing? The worse you are, the better it will be.' Believe me, folks, I was plenty 'worse.' Can you imagine? My musical debut—can't carry a tune and singing on a picture with Frank Sinatra, Dean Martin, Sammy Davis, and Bing Crosby."

—Peter Falk (costar, *Robin and the 7 Hoods*)

ABOVE With costar Bing Crosby, *Robin and the 7 Hoods*. **OPPOSITE** Color test, *Robin and the 7 Hoods*.

"It marks Frank Sinatra's debut as a director.... [His] style is straightforward and understated. It is to his credit that he tackled a serious subject on his first try when he could have taken the easy way out with still another gathering of The Clan...."

—Kevin Thomas
(*Los Angeles Times*, review, *None but the Brave*, 1965)

ABOVE One-sheet poster, *None but the Brave*.

"The toughest thing I had to do on the first day of shooting was to say, 'Print.' It took me ten minutes, because I liked the take, but I figured the minute I say, 'Print,' I'm on the record....It was in some ways tougher than I had thought. The director has so many things to worry about—pace, wardrobe, performance.... Next time I won't try to perform when I direct."

—Frank Sinatra

Directing, on location, *None but the Brave*.

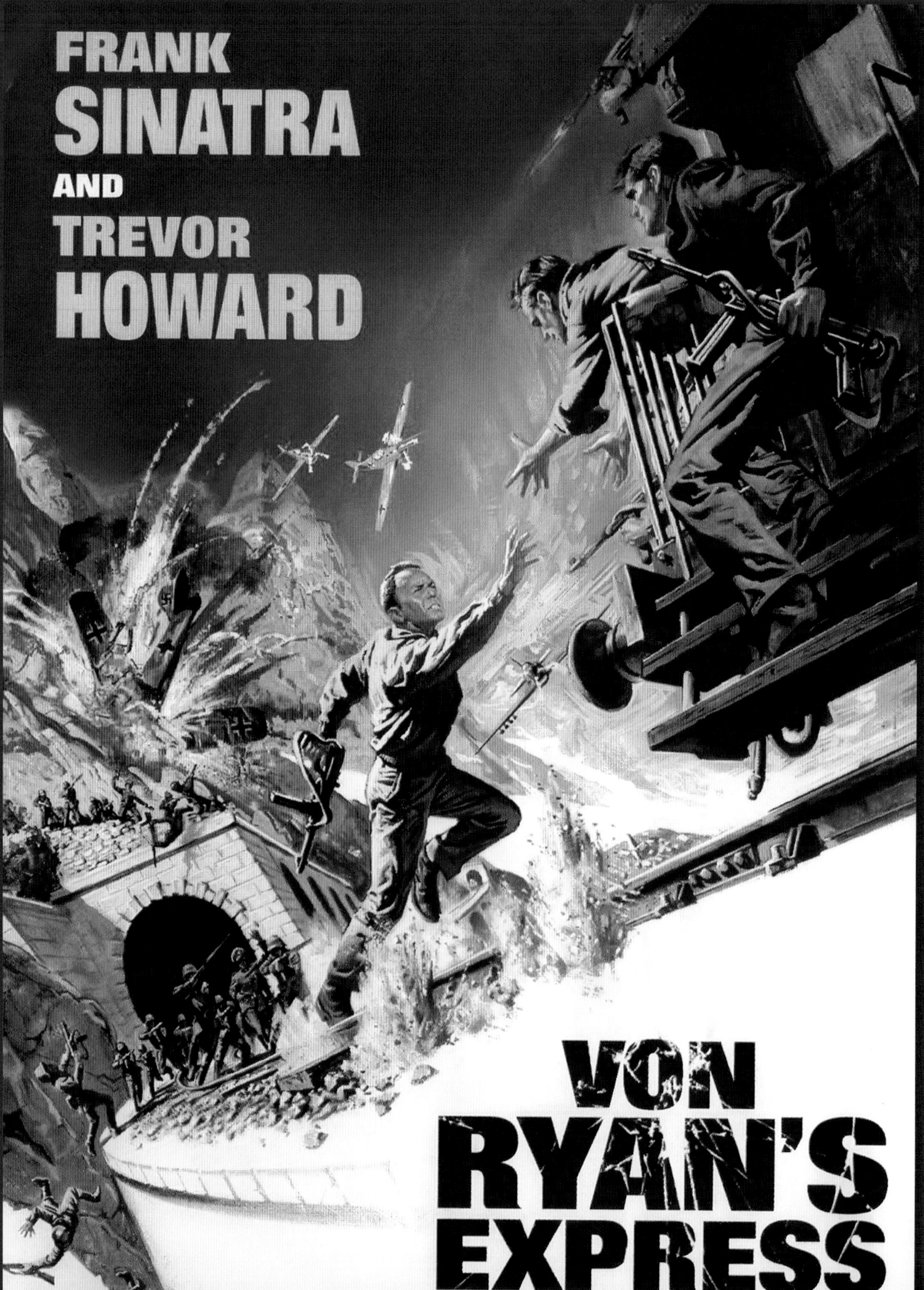
FRANK
SINATRA
AND
TREVOR
HOWARD
VON
RYAN'S
EXPRESS

"As the steely-eyed, curt American officer who takes command as an unpopular chief, Frank Sinatra underplays his role neatly and purposefully where it might easily have led him into an overdramatic trap.... It's a tough assignment, but he makes it believable, even at the finale where he is unwittingly sacrificed in staving off a final Nazi assault on the escape train.... This is Sinatra at his best as an actor, and far removed from his image as a rollicking, elbow-bending song stylist."

—Abe Greenberg
(*Hollywood Citizen-News*, review, *Von Ryan's Express*, 1965)

OPPOSITE One-sheet poster, *Von Ryan's Express*, 1965.

On location in Spain, *Von Ryan's Express*.

"Frank Sinatra had an extraordinary aura—with his piercing blue eyes. He was more than I expected. He was very professional. He'd walk in and everyone would go quiet. He was not overly gregarious, and he always had folk around him, so he was not approachable. Frank would arrive in a helicopter. He'd step out, do the scenes that were set up for him, and he'd be in and out in an hour! On one occasion Frank called out, 'Hey, where are you gonna get this [film] developed? Schwab's?'"

—John Leyton (costar, *Von Ryan's Express*)

OPPOSITE As Col. Joseph L. Ryan, *Von Ryan's Express*.

BY TINA SINATRA

Like all kids, I grew up thinking my dad could do anything. Well, maybe not anything—but I had the impression he was someone extraordinary. He was everywhere on radio and television, and I could even make him come alive on the little phonograph in my bedroom. "He's the greatest," I'd hear. "There's no one like him." If that's what everyone was saying, I assumed it was true. But I didn't really understand why.

In 1956, when I was eight years old, I saw Dad perform live at the Sands Hotel in Las Vegas—and I finally got it. His presence filled that darkened room. I was struck most of all by his ease and self-confidence; he seemed to be enjoying the fact that all eyes were on him. (I couldn't imagine doing what Dad did! Unlike my siblings, I had terrible stage fright.) For the first time, I began to understand the enormity of my father's talent and his command of his audience. I would never forget that night.

It was just about that time that I first saw my dad in a movie. The film was *The Kissing Bandit*, a forgettable musical made in 1948, the year I was born. I couldn't know he was playing a crooning composite of Zorro and Don Juan, but I knew he was adorable. Later I would learn it was one of several parts Pop would have passed on, sombrero and all, had he been given the option. At the time, Louis B. Mayer, then head of MGM, was calling the shots for all the studio's contract players. No doubt it was driving Dad nuts! He was longing to move from musicals to drama, but first he'd have to endure a priest's robe (in *The Miracle of the Bells*, 1948), a 1900s baseball hat (in *Take Me Out to the Ball Game*, 1949), and one more sailor's cap in the classic *On the Town*.

In 1953, everything changed with *From Here to Eternity*, which would win Dad a competitive Oscar. He followed it by donning his signature Cavanagh fedora in *Young at Heart*, and assumed his lasting place in American pop culture.

Mom had a rating system long before the MPAA, which meant I couldn't see *From Here to Eternity*, *Suddenly*, or *The Man With the Golden Arm*. But the system broke down in 1957, when she unwittingly took us to *The Joker Is Wild*. Pop played comedian and singer Joe E. Lewis, who gets his throat slashed early in the film—the sight of which sent me running hysterically out of the theater with my mother in close pursuit. She had to get Dad on the phone so I could hear his voice to believe he was okay.

Eventually I caught up with all of Dad's movies, and I have many personal favorites. But on one level I'm still that eight-year-old kid, amazed by his confidence to do it in the first place. My father was America's number-one pop male vocalist when Hollywood beckoned, and yet he dove headfirst, without a single acting lesson, into the most competitive business on the planet! But that was always my dad's way. He was fearlessly willing to take any risks necessary to compete for better parts in better films. Whether he was a sailor on twenty-four-hour leave in New York, or dragging a cannon across Spain, or commandeering a Nazi locomotive, or solving one last case as an aging detective, my dad gave his all.

In the early sixties, Pop still had more new things to try. He created a record label, formed a film and television production company, and even directed a movie. (Of the latter he said: Once was enough!) I must also add that Pop was a gifted and intuitive storyteller. This was an invaluable asset that proved to serve him well in all aspects of his career.

I followed in Dad's producing footsteps. In 1995, he did me the great honor of a guest appearance in a CBS movie-of-the-week called *Young at Heart* (no relation to the '54 version). It would be his last film role. As always, he was adorable.

Grauman's Chinese Theater, July 20, 1965.

"It was so much fun, a joke, and all quite ludicrous. Frank would come in one morning and say, 'We don't need this scene!' and just tear it out of the script and throw it away."

—Deborah Kerr (costar, *Marriage on the Rocks*, 1965)

ABOVE With costars Dean Martin and Deborah Kerr, *Marriage on the Rocks*, 1965. **OPPOSITE** With costar Joi Lansing. **OVERLEAF** As Dan Edwards, *Marriage on the Rocks*. Photo by Bob Willoughby.

"...the cameras were rolling again, Virna Lisi was leaning toward Sinatra in the sand, and then he pulled her down close to him. The camera now moved in for a close-up of their faces, ticking away for a few long seconds, but Sinatra and Lisi did not stop kissing, they just lay together in the sand wrapped in one another's arms, and then Virna Lisi's leg just slightly began to rise a bit, and everybody in the studio now watched in silence, not saying anything until [director] Donohue finally called out: 'If you ever get through, let me know. I'm running out of film.'"

—Gay Talese
(from the essay "Frank Sinatra Has a Cold," *Esquire* magazine, April 1966, about the filming of *Assault on a Queen*, 1966)

OPPOSITE One-sheet poster, *Assault on a Queen*, 1966. **RIGHT** Lobby cards.

ABOVE One-sheet and half-sheet posters, *The Naked Runner*, 1967. **RIGHT** *The Naked Runner*.

March 28, 1966

CAPTION

Frank Sinatra and director Sidney Furie got together in New York to go
over plans for filming THE NAKED RUNNER, Francis Clifford novel published
by Coward-McCann this month. Sinatra will star for his own production
company, Artanis Productions, and filming will take place on location in
Germany, Finland, and England this summer. The star and director will
begin scouting locations in early April.

"Of Sinatra, it must be said that even in this undemonstrative rendition of undistinguished material, he commands the screen. Given the plot there must have been a temptation to shout, moan, and chew the scenery. He put the temptation down, way down, and understates his histrionics. There is a sense of power held in check...."

—Charles Champlin
(*Los Angeles Times*, review, *The Naked Runner*, 1967)

OPPOSITE With director Sidney Furie, *The Naked Runner*. ABOVE As Sam Laker, *The Naked Runner*.

"*Tony Rome* is lively and entertaining and for this we must thank both the capable Mr. Sinatra and the persistent ghost of Mr. Bogart....Frank Sinatra has been a talent in search of a role ever since *The Manchurian Candidate*, and, at last, in *Tony Rome*, he has found himself one."

—Hollis Alpert (*Saturday Review*, review, *Tony Rome*, 1967)

OPPOSITE One-sheet poster, *Tony Rome*, 1967.

20th CENTURY-FOX
Presents
frank sinatra
is tony rome
THE ACTION
IS SO FAST...
IT'S A WONDER
TONY ROME
STAYS ALIVE....
AND SINGLE!
Co-Starring JILL ST. JOHN · RICHARD CONTE · GENA ROWLANDS · SIMON OAKLAND
JEFFREY LYNN · LLOYD BOCHNER and SUE LYON as Diana · Produced by Aaron
Rosenberg · Directed by Gordon Douglas · Screenplay by Richard Breen
Hear Nancy Sinatra
sing the title song!
Based on the Novel "Miami Mayhem" by Marvin H. Albert · PANAVISION® · COLOR BY DE LUXE An Arcola-Millfield Productions Picture

"For those who like their screen detective recognizable and raw, and their mystery melodramas seamy and colloquial, this thing with Mr. Sinatra should satisfy their taste. It is brassy, trashy, vulgar and Miami Beach colorful."

—Bosley Crowther (*The New York Times*, review, *Tony Rome*)

On location in Miami, with
director Gordon Douglas and
costar Jill St. John, *Tony Rome*.

"Sinatra is always an interesting actor...and in *The Detective* he has mellowed into a genuinely convincing cop. He is weary and wise and tough and cynical in the way Bogart used to be, and indeed he is probably better at these hard-boiled roles than anyone since Bogart died."

—Rogert Ebert (*Chicago Sun-Times*, review, *The Detective*, 1968)

OPPOSITE One sheet poster, *The Detective*, 1968. OVERLEAF With costar Lee Remick, *The Detective*. Lobby cards.

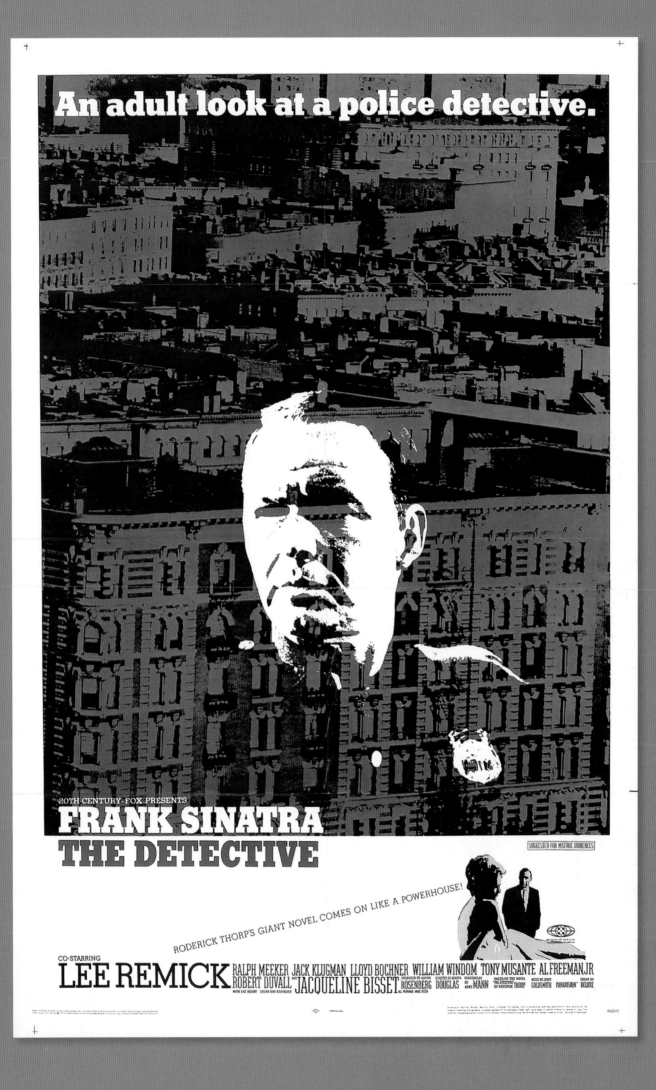

s the most raw talent and magnetism
man I've met. While we were filming,
was working at the Fontainebleau, and
a complete revelation to see him in front
audience. To completely hold people the
e did is a remarkable thing."

Welch (costar, *Lady in Cement*, 1968)

ABOVE With costar Raquel Welch, *Lady in Cement*, 1968.
OPPOSITE One-sheet poster, *Lady in Cement*.

"I had been continually rehearsing a scene with a young actress who had little experience and understandably was nervous. Frank, who was to be in the scene later, had the sensitivity to see it. He knew his being around would only make her more nervous, so he disappeared to the back of the set. I was concerned how the shooting of this scene would come across. Frank came over to me and said, 'Relax, she'll be fine.' And to top it all off, he did a little prophesying. 'She's also going to be a big star.' At that time I could not see it. But I'm sure that actress, who goes by the name of Raquel Welch, will forgive me."

—Gordon Douglas (director, *Lady in Cement*)

On set, *Lady in Cement*, 1968.

"Sinatra's Tony Rome is a fusion of insouciance, cynicism, battered but surviving idealism, wisecrackery, courage, libido, thirst, and all the more interesting hungers. He clearly enjoys the role."

—Charles Champlin
(*Los Angeles Times*, review, *Lady in Cement*)

ABOVE AND OPPOSITE As Tony Rome, *Lady in Cement*.

"I was a stage-struck bobby soxer when he was singing at the Paramount in New York City. I remained a tongue-tied fan of his....He was such a gifted singer— and then grew into a fine actor...I just remember having fun working with him. He's a very generous man... and has never outgrown his ability to beguile."

—Anne Jackson
(costar, *Dirty Dingus Magee*, 1970)

On location in Tucson, Arizona, *Dirty Dingus Magee*, 1970.

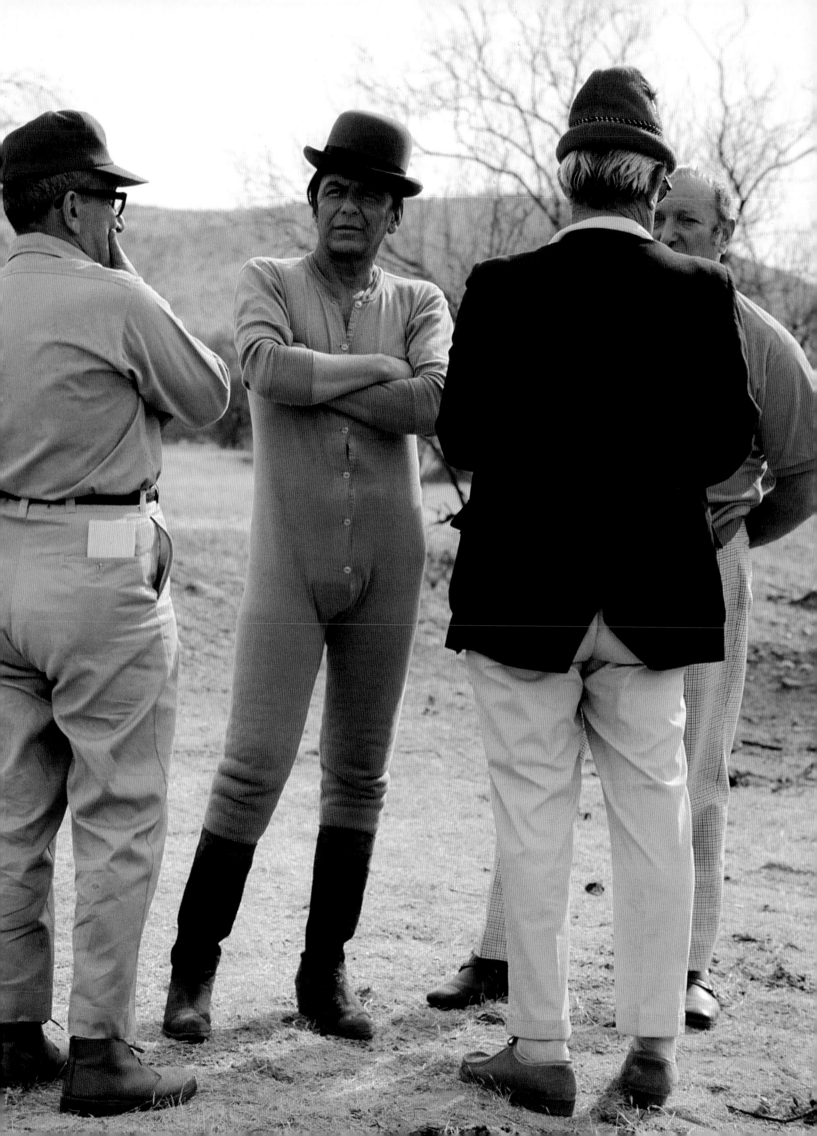

…Sinatra plays this role close to his chest, and looks and acts very touchingly like a tired old cop on the threshold of retirement. We can sympathize with him, and that's partly because he resists any temptation to give us a reprise of those wisecracking wise-asses he played in the 1960s. This is a new performance, built from the ground up."

—Roger Ebert
(*Chicago Sun-Times*, review, *The First Deadly Sin*, 1980)

THE FIRST DEADLY SIN

PHOTO CREDITS

Author's Collection
Endpapers, pages 30, 38, 40, 41, 50, 51, 52, 54, 59, 60, 64, 65, 83, 96, 104, 107, 120, 121, 127, 129, 148, 149, 160, 165, 169, 180, 186, 197, 198, 217, 218, 219, 228, 229, 251, 255, 259, 262, 276, 277, 278, 283, 289, 291, 293.

© Bob Willoughby / MPTV (mptvimages.com)
Pages 199, 274/275.

Courtesy Everett Collection
Pages 116/117, 171, 174, 188/189, 216, 248, 249, 272, 300.

Courtesy Independent Visions
Cover, Pages 2/3, 29, 30/31, 36/37, 39, 45, 46, 47, 48/49, 53, 60/61, 62, 63, 67, 71, 72, 74/75, 77, 78, 79, 90/91, 98/99, 100, 101, 108/109, 110, 111, 112/113, 114, 130, 131, 134, 135, 136/137, 138, 139, 142, 143, 144, 145, 151, 156/157, 158, 160/161, 162, 163, 181, 183, 185, 191, 192/193, 194/195, 202/203, 212/213, 215, 220, 222/223, 224, 225, 226/227, 230/231, 231, 232, 233, 234, 234/235, 236, 237, 238, 239, 240/241, 242, 243, 244, 244/245, 256, 257, 258, 260/261, 264/265, 270/271, 273, 278/279, 280, 281, 296.

Courtesy Photofest (photofestnyc.com)
Pages 26/27, 28, 34, 35, 37, 42, 43, 55, 58, 68/69, 73, 76, 81, 82, 85, 93, 94/95, 97, 102/103, 105, 106, 115, 118/119, 128, 132/133, 140, 146/147, 150, 159, 172, 175, 176, 178/179, 182, 196, 201, 204, 206/207, 208, 211, 214, 246/247, 250, 252/253, 254, 266, 284, 285, 290/291, 294, 301.

© Sid Avery / MPTV (mptvimages.com)
Pages 177, 204/205.

The Kobal Collection / Art Resource (picture-desk.com)
Pages 56, 57, 70, 122/123, 154, 166/167, 168, 286/287, 292, 297, 298/299.

The Lou Valentino Collection
Pages 32, 33, 44.

© Zinn Arthur / The Image Works (theimageworks.com)
Pages 152/153, 173.

REFERENCES

5001 Nights at the Movies, Pauline Kael. Henry Holt & Co. New York, 1991.

All the Way: A Biography of Frank Sinatra, Michael Freedland. Weidenfeld & Nicolson, London, 1997.

Ann Miller: Tops in Taps, Jim Connor. Franklin Watts. New York, 1981.

Awake in the Dark: The Best of Roger Ebert: Forty Years of Reviews, Essays and Interviews, Roger Ebert. University of Chicago Press. Chicago, 2006.

Balancing Act: The Unauthorized Biography of Angela Lansbury, Martin Gottfried. Little Brown & Co. Boston, 1999.

Betty Garrett and Other Songs: A Life on Stage and Screen, Betty Garrett with Ron Rapoport. Madison Books. Lanham NY, 1998.

Charles Walters: The Director Who Made Hollywood Dance, Brent Phillips. University Press of Kentucky. Lexington, 2014.

The Cinema History of Burt Lancaster, David Fury. Artist's Press. Minneapolis MN, 1989.

The Cinema of Sinatra: The Actor, On Screen and In Song, Scott Allen Nollen. Luminary Press. Baltimore MD, 2003.

Dance While You Can, Shirley MacLaine. Bantam Books. New York, 1991.

The Defiant One: A Biography of Tony Curtis, Anthony Malone. McFarland & Co. Jefferson NC, 2013.

Directed by Vincente Minnelli, Stephen Harvey. MOMA/Harper & Row. New York, 1989.

Dino: The Dean Martin Story, Michael Freedland. W. H. Allen. London, 1984.

Dino: Living High in the Dirty Business of Dreams, Nick Tosches. Doubleday. New York, 1992.

Doris Day: Her Own Story, A. E. Hotchner. William Morrow & Co. New York, 1976.

Doris Day: The Untold Story of the Girl Next Door, David Kaufman. Virgin Books. New York, 2008.

Faye Dunaway, Allan Hunter. St. Martin's Press. New York, 1986.

The Films of Frank Sinatra, Gene Ringgold and Clifford McCarty. Citadel Press. New York, 1989.

The Films of Kirk Douglas, Tony Thomas. Citadel Press. New York, 1991.

Frank Sinatra, John Howlett. Courage Books. Philadelphia, 1980.

Frank Sinatra, John Frayn Turner. Taylor Trade Publishing. Dallas, 2004.

Frank Sinatra: An American Legend, Nancy Sinatra. General Publishing Group Inc. Santa Monica CA, 1995.

The Frank Sinatra Film Guide, Daniel O'Brien. B. T. Batsford. London, 1998.

Frank: The Voice, James Kaplan. Doubleday. New York, 2010.

Fred Zinnemann: Interviews, Gabriel Miller, ed. University Press of Mississippi. Jackson, 2000.

Gene Kelly: A Life of Dance and Dreams, Alvin Yudkoff. Backstage Books. New York, 1999.

The Good, the Bad, and Me: In My Anecdotage, Eli Wallach. Harcourt Inc. Orlando FL, 2005.

The Great Movies, William Bayer. Grosset & Dunlap. New York, 1973.

Groucho: The Life and Times of Julius Henry Marx, Stefan Kanfer. Alfred A. Knopf. New York, 2000.

Hollywood in a Suitcase, Sammy Davis, Jr. William Morrow & Co. New York, 1980.

Hollywood Musicals, Ted Sennett. Harry N. Abrams. New York, 1981.

In Black and White: The Life of Sammy Davis, Jr., Wil Haygood. Alfred A. Knopf. New York, 2003.

Jane Russell: An Autobiography—My Path and My Detours, Jane Russell. Franklin Watts, Inc. New York, 2006.

John Frankenheimer: Interviews, Essays, and Profiles, Stephen B. Armstrong, ed. The Scarecrow Press Inc. Toronto, 2013.

Just One More Thing: Stories from My Life, Peter Falk. Carroll & Graf Publishers. New York, 2006.

Kim Novak: On Camera, Larry Kleno. A. S. Barnes & Co. San Diego CA, 1980.

Kim Novak: Reluctant Goddess, Peter Harry Brown. St. Martin's Press New York, 1986.

Leading Men of MGM, Joan Ellen Wayne. Carroll & Graf Publishers. New York, 2005.

A Mad Mad Mad Mad World: A Life in Hollywood, Stanley Kramer with

Thomas M. Coffey. Harcourt Brace & Co. New York, 1997.

A Man and His Art: Frank Sinatra, Tina Sinatra, ed. Random House. New York, 1991.

McQueen: The Biography, Christopher Sandford. Taylor Trade Publishing. New York, 2003.

Mitchum: In His Own Words, Jerry Roberts, ed. Limelight Editions. New York, 2000.

Natasha: The Biography of Natalie Wood, Suzanne Finstad. Harmony Books. New York, 2001.

The New Biographical Dictionary of Film, David Thomson. Alfred A. Knopf. New York, 2002.

Otto Preminger: The Man Who Would Be King, Foster Hirsch. Alfred A. Knopf. New York, 2007.

Peter Lawford: The Man Who Kept the Secrets, James Spada. Bantam Books. New York, 1991.

The Peter Lawford Story: Life with the Kennedys, Monroe, and the Rat Pack, Patricia Seaton Lawford with Ted Schwarz. Carroll & Graf Publishers. New York, 1988.

Pieces of My Heart: A Life, Robert J. Wagner with Scott Eyman. HarperCollins. New York, 2008.

The Ragman's Son: An Autobiography, Kirk Douglas. Simon & Schuster. New York, 1988.

Raquel Welch: Sex Symbol to Super Star, Peter Haining. St. Martin's Press. New York, 1984.

Remembering Sinatra; A Life in Pictures, Robert Sullivan and Life eds. Life Books. New York, 1998.

Robert Mitchum: Baby, I Don't Care, Lee Server. St. Martin's Press. New York, 2001.

Sammy: An Autobiography, Sammy Davis, Jr., with Jane and Burt Boyar. Farrar Straus & Giroux. New York, 2000.

Sinatra, Richard Havers. Dorling Kindersley, London, 2004.

Sinatra, Robin Douglas-Home. Michael Joseph. London, 1962.

Sinatra: Behind the Legend, J. Randy Taraborrelli. Birch Lane Press. Secaucus NJ, 1997.

Sinatra: Hollywood His Way, Timothy Knight. Running Press. Philadelphia, 2010.

Sinatra in Hollywood, Tom Santopietro. St. Martin's Press. New York, 2006.

Sinatra: The Life, Anthony Summers and Robbyn Swan. Alfred A. Knopf. New York, 2005.

Sinatra: A Portrait of the Artist, Ray Coleman. Turner Publishing Inc. Atlanta GA, 1995.

Sophia Loren: A Biography, Warren G. Harris. Simon & Schuster. New York, 1998.

Sophia Loren: Living and Loving: Her Own Story, A. E. Hotchner. William Morrow & Co. New York, 1979.

Spencer Tracy, Larry Swindell. World Publishing Co. Cleveland OH, 1969.

Spencer Tracy: A Biography, James Curtis. Alfred A. Knopf. New York, 2011.

Steve McQueen: A Biography, Marc Eliot. Crown/Archetype. New York, 2011.

Tony Curtis: The Autobiography, Tony Curtis and Barry Paris. William Morrow & Co. New York, 1993.

Tony Curtis: The Man and His Movies, Allan Hunter. St. Martin's Press. New York, 1985.

True Grace: The Life and Times of an American Princess, Wendy Leigh. St. Martin's Press. New York, 2007.

Unsinkable: A Memoir, Debbie Reynolds and Dorrian Hannaway. William Morrow & Co. New York, 2013.

Vincente Minnelli: Hollywood's Dark Dreamer, Emanuel Levy. St. Martin's Press. New York, 2009.

The Way You Wear Your Hat: Frank Sinatra and the Lost Art of Livin', Bill Zehme. HarperCollins. New York, 1997.

When Frankie Went to Hollywood, Frank Sinatra and American Male Identity, Karen McNally. University of Illinois Press. Urbana/Chicago, 1998.

Why Sinatra Matters, Pete Hamill. Little Brown & Co. Boston, 1998.

You Must Remember This: Life & Style in Hollywood's Golden Age, Robert J. Wagner with Scott Eyman. Viking,. New York, 2014.

"Frank Sinatra Has a Cold," Gay Talese, *Esquire*. Esquire Inc., New York, April 1966.

"Khruschchev in Hollywood," Peter Carlson, *Smithsonian*. Washington DC, July 2009.

"Meeting at the Summit: Sinatra and His Buddies Bust 'Em Up in Vegas," Robert LeGare, *Playboy*. HMH Publishing Corp., Chicago, June 1960.

"The Word on Frank Sinatra," *Playboy*. HMH Publishing Corp., Chicago, November 1958.

imdb.com   reviewjournal.com
newsweek.com   time.com
playboy.com   variety.com
pophistory.com   youtube.com
rottentomatoes.com

ACKNOWLEDGMENTS

Special thanks to:

Amanda Erlinger

Nancy Sinatra, Tina Sinatra, and Frank Sinatra, Jr.

Jimmy Edwards and Kelly Spinks at Frank Sinatra Enterprises.

Stan Corwin

Sally Richardson, Jennifer Weis, Sylvan Creekmore, Ellis B. Levine, and the team at St. Martin's Press.

Evan Macdonald and Sloan De Forest.

Manoah Bowman, Andrew Howick, Howard Mandelbaum, Matt Severson, Lou Valentino, and Jamie Vuignier.

Russell Adams, Susan Bernard, Chris Cordone, Lauretta Dives, Michael Epstein, Laura Ex, Lorraine Goonan, Todd Ifft, Glenn Kawahara, Dave Kent, Jeffrey McCall, Edie Shaw Marcus, Alan Mercer, Julie Newmar, Mauricio Padilha, Roger Padilha, Alison Jo Rigney, Loretta Schmidt, Reynold Schmidt, Scott Schwimer, Ramona Sliva, Melissa Stevens, Meta Shaw Stevens, Jill St. John, Debra Tate, Jeff Thompson, Victory Tischler-Blue, Isabel Torres, Robert J. Wagner, Raquel Welch, Fay Wills, Ralph Wills.

Front-of-jacket photograph: *A Hole in the Head* (1959). Courtesy Independent Visions.
Back-of-jacket photographs (clockwise from top left): *Anchors Aweigh* (1945). Courtesy Photofest. *The Manchurian
Candidate* (1962), *From Here to Eternity* (1953), and *The Naked Runner* (1967). Courtesy Independent Visions.
David Wills photo by Alan Mercer. Stephen Schmidt photo by Isabel Torres. Amanda Erlinger photo by Michael Erlinger.